Sing out your
thanks to the LORD....
He...makes the grass grow
in mountain pastures.

PSALM 147:7–8

Our Daily Bread.
DEVOTIONAL BIBLE

DISCOVERY HOUSE
PUBLISHERS®

Feeding the Soul with the Word of God

New Living
Translation®
SECOND EDITION

Tyndale House Publishers, Inc.
Carol Stream, Illinois

CONTENTS

Introduction to the
OUR DAILY BREAD DEVOTIONAL BIBLE

From prison cells to dinner tables to bedroom nightstands, *Our Daily Bread* can be found in countless locations in dozens of countries across the globe. Offering food for the soul, this "little book," as many people refer to it, has found its way into the hearts and lives of multiple millions of people since Radio Bible Class published the first edition in April 1956.

Everywhere *Our Daily Bread* goes and in any of the more than thirty languages into which it is translated, the booklet points readers to the joy of living not by bread alone, but by the love and faithfulness of our Provider God.

From the beginning, since Henry Bosch and Dr. M. R. DeHaan put together that first edition of *Our Daily Bread* in the middle of the twentieth century, the writers have used stories to capture readers' interest and point them to the overarching story of the Bible and the wisdom within its pages. The partnership between the New Living Translation of the Bible and *Our Daily Bread* is a natural extension of the desire to make the wisdom of the Bible understandable and accessible to all. As you explore the passages that accompany each *Our Daily Bread* article, we trust that you will find divinely inspired words that renew your love and enthusiasm for the living Word of God.

Our Daily Bread is designed to be a companion resource for your personal times with God. Each day it introduces a thought from the Bible to give you reason for deeper devotion to the God who has first loved us. Imagine how the Lord can be honored if each day you capture one grand truth from His Word and allow it—with the help of the Holy Spirit—to become an integral part of your day-to-day existence. Imagine how continuing to discover such love and help could change your life!

Our Daily Bread helps us find guidance for troubled times, health for our spiritual condition, and hope for a blessed future. The writers of *Our Daily Bread* urge readers to go into each new day with confidence in God, who promises us: "I will guide you along the best pathway for your life. I will advise you and watch over you" (Psalm 32:8).

Without a connection to the eternal truths of the Bible, the words of *Our Daily Bread* would mean nothing. Yes, the stories would still be genuine, and they would portray unique glimpses of life as we know it. Indeed, the lessons presented might even be helpful. But unless the lessons and principles of the booklet are taken directly from God's inspired Book, they would have no lasting value.

So, it is our prayer that as you open your Bible and seek its infinite truth, you can use the articles from this "little book" to assist you as you seek a stronger relationship with Jesus and explore the eternal, matchless wisdom of the God-breathed words of "the Book."

RBC Ministries

A NOTE TO READERS

The *Holy Bible,* New Living Translation, was first published in 1996. It quickly became one of the most popular Bible translations in the English-speaking world. While the NLT's influence was rapidly growing, the Bible Translation Committee determined that an additional investment in scholarly review and text refinement could make it even better. So shortly after its initial publication, the committee began an eight-year process with the purpose of increasing the level of the NLT's precision without sacrificing its easy-to-understand quality. This second-generation text was completed in 2004, with minor changes subsequently introduced in 2007.

The goal of any Bible translation is to convey the meaning and content of the ancient Hebrew, Aramaic, and Greek texts as accurately as possible to contemporary readers. The challenge for our translators was to create a text that would communicate as clearly and powerfully to today's readers as the original texts did to readers and listeners in the ancient biblical world. The resulting translation is easy to read and understand, while also accurately communicating the meaning and content of the original biblical texts. The NLT is a general-purpose text especially good for study, devotional reading, and reading aloud in worship services.

We believe that the New Living Translation—which combines the latest biblical scholarship with a clear, dynamic writing style—will communicate God's word powerfully to all who read it. We publish it with the prayer that God will use it to speak his timeless truth to the church and the world in a fresh, new way.

Tyndale House Publishers
October 2007

Introduction to the
NEW LIVING TRANSLATION

Translation Philosophy and Methodology

English Bible translations tend to be governed by one of two general translation theories. The first theory has been called "formal-equivalence," "literal," or "word-for-word" translation. According to this theory, the translator attempts to render each word of the original language into English and seeks to preserve the original syntax and sentence structure as much as possible in translation. The second theory has been called "dynamic-equivalence," "functional-equivalence," or "thought-for-thought" translation. The goal of this translation theory is to produce in English the closest natural equivalent of the message expressed by the original-language text, both in meaning and in style.

Both of these translation theories have their strengths. A formal-equivalence translation preserves aspects of the original text—including ancient idioms, term consistency, and original-language syntax—that are valuable for scholars and professional study. It allows a reader to trace formal elements of the original-language text through the English translation. A dynamic-equivalence translation, on the other hand, focuses on translating the message of the original-language text. It ensures that the meaning of the text is readily apparent to the contemporary reader. This allows the message to come through with immediacy, without requiring the reader to struggle with foreign idioms and awkward syntax.

The translators of the New Living Translation set out to render the message of the original texts of Scripture into clear, contemporary English. As they did so, they kept the concerns of both formal-equivalence and dynamic-equivalence in mind. On the one hand, they translated as simply and literally as possible when that approach yielded an accurate, clear, and natural English text. Many words and phrases were rendered literally and consistently into English, preserving essential literary and rhetorical devices, ancient metaphors, and word choices that give structure to the text and provide echoes of meaning from one passage to the next.

On the other hand, the translators rendered the message more dynamically when the literal rendering was hard to understand, was misleading, or yielded archaic or foreign wording. They clarified difficult metaphors and terms to aid in the reader's understanding. The translators first struggled with the meaning of the words and phrases in the ancient context; then they rendered the message into clear, natural English. Their goal was to be both faithful to the ancient texts and eminently readable.

Translation Process and Team

To produce an accurate translation of the Bible into contemporary English, the translation team needed the skills necessary to enter into the thought patterns of the ancient authors and then to render their ideas, connotations, and effects into clear, contemporary English. To begin this process, qualified biblical scholars were needed to interpret the meaning of the original text and to check it against our base English translation. In order to guard against personal and theological biases, the scholars needed to represent a diverse group of evangelicals who would employ the best exegetical tools. Then to work alongside the scholars, skilled English stylists were needed to shape the text into clear, contemporary English.

With these concerns in mind, the Bible Translation Committee recruited teams of scholars that represented a broad spectrum of denominations, theological perspectives, and backgrounds within the worldwide evangelical community. Each book of the Bible was assigned to three different scholars with proven expertise in the book or group of books to be reviewed. Each of these scholars made a thorough review of a base translation and submitted suggested revisions to the appropriate Senior Translator. The Senior Translator then reviewed and summarized these suggestions and proposed a first-draft revision of the base text. This draft served as the basis for several additional phases of exegetical and stylistic committee review. Then the Bible Translation Committee jointly reviewed and approved every verse of the final translation.

The New Living Translation was first published in 1996. Shortly after its initial publication, the Bible Translation Committee began a process of further committee review and translation refinement. The purpose of this continued revision was to increase the level of precision without sacrificing the text's easy-to-understand quality. This second-edition text was completed in 2004, with minor changes subsequently introduced in 2007.

The Texts behind the New Living Translation

The Old Testament translators used the Masoretic Text of the Hebrew Bible as represented in *Biblia Hebraica Stuttgartensia* (1977), with its extensive system of textual notes. The translators also took into account the Dead Sea Scrolls, the Septuagint and other Greek manuscripts, the Samaritan Pentateuch, the Syriac Peshitta, the Latin Vulgate, and any other versions or manuscripts that shed light on difficult passages.

The New Testament translators used the two standard editions of the Greek New Testament: the *Greek New Testament*, published by the United Bible Societies (UBS, fourth revised edition, 1993), and *Novum Testamentum Graece*, edited by Nestle and Aland (NA, twenty-seventh edition, 1993). These two editions, which have the same text but differ in punctuation and textual notes, represent, for the most part, the best in modern textual scholarship. However, in cases where strong textual or other scholarly evidence supported the decision, the translators sometimes chose to differ from the UBS and NA Greek texts and followed variant readings found in other ancient witnesses. Significant textual variants of this sort are always noted in the textual notes of the New Living Translation.

Translation Issues

The translators have made a conscious effort to provide a text that can be easily understood by the typical reader of modern English. To this end, we sought to use only vocabulary and language structures in common use today. We avoided using language likely to become quickly dated or that reflects only a narrow subdialect of English, with the goal of making the New Living Translation as broadly useful and timeless as possible.

But our concern for readability goes beyond the concerns of vocabulary and sentence structure. We are also concerned about historical and cultural barriers to understanding the Bible, and we have sought to translate terms shrouded in history and culture in ways that can be immediately understood. To this end:

- We have converted ancient weights and measures (for example, "ephah" [a unit of dry volume] or "cubit" [a unit of length]) to modern English (American) equivalents, since the ancient measures are not generally meaningful to today's readers. (In the textual footnotes we offer the literal Hebrew, Aramaic, or Greek measures, along with modern metric equivalents. The same general principle of giving the literal in a footnote was also applied to the other issues listed below.)
- Instead of translating ancient currency values literally, we have expressed them in common terms that communicate the message. For example, in the Old Testament, "ten shekels of silver" becomes "ten pieces of silver" to convey the intended message.
- Since the names of Hebrew months are unknown to most contemporary readers, and since the Hebrew lunar calendar fluctuates from year to year in relation to the solar calendar used today, we have looked for clear ways to communicate the time of year the Hebrew months (such as Abib) refer to. Where it is possible to define a specific ancient date in terms of our modern calendar, we use modern dates in the text. A textual footnote then gives the literal Hebrew date and states the rationale for our rendering. (See, for example, the text and note at Ezra 6:15.)
- Since ancient references to the time of day differ from our modern methods of denoting time, we have used renderings that are instantly understandable to the modern reader. Accordingly, we have rendered specific times of day by using approximate equivalents in terms of our common "o'clock" system.
- When the meaning of a proper name (or a wordplay inherent in a proper name) is relevant to the message of the text, its meaning is often illuminated with a textual footnote. For example, in Exodus 2:10 the text reads: "The princess named him Moses, for she explained, 'I lifted him out of the water.' " The accompanying footnote reads: "*Moses* sounds like a Hebrew term that means 'to lift out.' "
- Many words and phrases carry a great deal of cultural meaning that was obvious to the original readers but needs explanation in our own culture. For example, the phrase "they beat their breasts" (Luke 23:48) in ancient times meant that people were very upset, often in mourning. In our translation we chose to translate this phrase dynamically for clarity: "They went home *in deep sorrow.*"

- Metaphorical language is sometimes difficult for contemporary readers to understand, so at times we have chosen to translate or illuminate the meaning of a metaphor. For example, the ancient poet writes, "Your neck is *like* the tower of David" (Song of Songs 4:4). We have rendered it "Your neck is *as beautiful as* the tower of David" to clarify the intended positive meaning of the simile.
- When the content of the original language text is poetic in character, we have rendered it in English poetic form. Hebrew poetry often uses parallelism, a literary form where a second phrase (or in some instances a third or fourth) echoes the initial phrase in some way. Whenever possible, we sought to represent these parallel phrases in natural poetic English.
- The Greek term *hoi Ioudaioi* is literally translated "the Jews" in many English translations. In the Gospel of John, however, this term doesn't always refer to the Jewish people generally. In some contexts, it refers more particularly to the Jewish religious leaders. We have attempted to capture the meaning in these different contexts by using terms such as "the people" (with a footnote: Greek *the Jewish people*) or "the religious leaders," where appropriate.
- One challenge we faced was how to translate accurately the ancient biblical text that was originally written in a context where male-oriented terms were used to refer to humanity generally. We needed to respect the nature of the ancient context while also trying to make the translation clear to a modern audience that tends to read male-oriented language as applying only to males. Often the original text, though using masculine terms, clearly intends that the message be applied to both men and women. A typical example is found in the New Testament letters, where the believers are called "brothers" (*adelphoi*). Yet it is clear from the content of these letters that they were addressed to all the believers—male and female. Thus, we have usually translated this Greek word as "brothers and sisters" in order to represent the historical situation more accurately.
- We should emphasize that all masculine nouns and pronouns used to represent God (for example, "Father") have been maintained without exception. All decisions of this kind have been driven by the concern to reflect accurately the intended meaning of the original texts of Scripture.

Lexical Consistency in Terminology

For the sake of clarity, we have translated certain original-language terms consistently, especially within synoptic passages and for commonly repeated rhetorical phrases, and within certain word categories such as divine names and non-theological technical terminology (e.g., liturgical, legal, cultural, zoological, and botanical terms). For theological terms, we have allowed a greater semantic range of acceptable English words or phrases for a single Hebrew or Greek word. We have avoided some theological terms that are not readily understood by many modern readers. For example, we avoided using words such as "justification" and "sanctification," which are carryovers from Latin translations. In place of these words, we have provided renderings such as "made right with God" and "made holy."

Many individuals in the Bible, especially the Old Testament, are known by more than one name (e.g., Uzziah/Azariah). For the sake of clarity, we have tried to use a single spelling for any one individual, footnoting the literal spelling whenever we differ from it. This is especially helpful in delineating the kings of Israel and Judah. King Joash/Jehoash of Israel has been consistently called Jehoash, while King Joash/Jehoash of Judah is called Joash. A similar distinction has been used to distinguish between Joram/Jehoram of Israel and Joram/Jehoram of Judah. All such decisions were made with the goal of clarifying the text for the reader. When the ancient biblical writers clearly had a theological purpose in their choice of a variant name (e.g., Esh-baal/Ishbosheth), the different names have been maintained with an explanatory footnote.

The Rendering of Divine Names

In the Old Testament, all appearances of 'el, 'elohim, or 'eloah have been translated "God," except where the context demands the translation "god(s)." We have generally rendered the tetragrammaton (YHWH) consistently as "the LORD," utilizing a form with small capitals that is common among English translations. This will distinguish it from the name 'adonai, which we render "Lord." When 'adonai and YHWH appear together, we have rendered it "Sovereign LORD." When 'elohim and YHWH appear together, we have rendered it "LORD God." When YH (the short form of YHWH) and YHWH appear together, we have rendered it "LORD GOD." When YHWH appears with the term tseba'oth, we have rendered it "LORD of Heaven's Armies" to translate the meaning of the name. In a few cases, we have utilized the transliteration, Yahweh, when the personal character of the name is being invoked in contrast to another divine name or the name of some other god (for example, see Exodus 3:15; 6:2-3).

In the Gospels and Acts, the Greek word christos has been translated as "Messiah" when the context assumes a Jewish audience. When a Gentile audience can be assumed (which is consistently the case in the Epistles and Revelation), christos has been translated as "Christ." The Greek word kurios is consistently translated "Lord," except that it is translated "LORD" wherever the New Testament text explicitly quotes from the Old Testament, and the text there has it in small capitals.

Textual Footnotes

The New Living Translation provides several kinds of textual footnotes, all designated in the text with an asterisk:

- When for the sake of clarity the NLT renders a difficult or potentially confusing phrase dynamically, we generally give the literal rendering in a textual footnote. This allows the reader to see the literal source of our dynamic rendering and how our translation relates to other more literal translations. These notes are prefaced with "Hebrew," "Aramaic," or "Greek," identifying the language of the underlying source text. For example, in Acts 2:42 we translated the literal "breaking of bread" (from the Greek) as "the Lord's Supper" to clarify that this verse refers to the ceremonial practice of the church rather than just an ordinary meal. Then we attached a footnote to "the Lord's Supper," which reads: "Greek *the breaking of bread.*"

- Textual footnotes are also used to show alternative renderings, prefaced with the word "Or." These normally occur for passages where an aspect of the meaning is debated. On occasion, we also provide notes on words or phrases that represent a departure from long-standing tradition. These notes are prefaced with "Traditionally rendered." For example, the footnote to the translation "serious skin disease" at Leviticus 13:2 says: "Traditionally rendered *leprosy.* The Hebrew word used throughout this passage is used to describe various skin diseases."

- When our translators follow a textual variant that differs significantly from our standard Hebrew or Greek texts (listed earlier), we document that difference with a footnote. We also footnote cases when the NLT excludes a passage that is included in the Greek text known as the *Textus Receptus* (and familiar to readers through its translation in the King James Version). In such cases, we offer a translation of the excluded text in a footnote, even though it is generally recognized as a later addition to the Greek text and not part of the original Greek New Testament.

- All Old Testament passages that are quoted in the New Testament are identified by a textual footnote at the New Testament location. When the New Testament clearly quotes from the Greek translation of the Old Testament, and when it differs significantly in wording from the Hebrew text, we also place a textual footnote at the Old Testament location. This note includes a rendering of the Greek version, along with a cross-reference to the New Testament passage(s) where it is cited (for example, see notes on Psalms 8:2; 53:3; Proverbs 3:12).

- Some textual footnotes provide cultural and historical information on places, things, and people in the Bible that are probably obscure to modern readers. Such notes should aid the reader in understanding the message of the text. For example, in Acts 12:1, "King Herod" is named in this translation as "King Herod Agrippa" and is identified in a footnote as being "the nephew of Herod Antipas and a grandson of Herod the Great."

- When the meaning of a proper name (or a wordplay inherent in a proper name) is relevant to the meaning of the text, it is either illuminated with a textual footnote or included within parentheses in the text itself. For example, the footnote concerning the name "Eve" at Genesis 3:20 reads: "*Eve* sounds like a Hebrew term that means 'to give life.' " This wordplay in the Hebrew illuminates the meaning of the text, which goes on to say that Eve "would be the mother of all who live."

AS WE SUBMIT this translation for publication, we recognize that any translation of the Scriptures is subject to limitations and imperfections. Anyone who has attempted to communicate the richness of God's Word into another language will realize it is impossible to make a perfect translation. Recognizing these limitations, we sought God's guidance and wisdom throughout this project. Now we pray that he will accept our efforts and use this translation for the benefit of the church and of all people.

We pray that the New Living Translation will overcome some of the barriers of history, culture, and language that have kept people from reading and understanding God's Word. We hope that readers unfamiliar with the Bible will find the words clear and easy to understand and that readers well versed in the Scriptures will gain a fresh perspective. We pray that readers will gain insight and wisdom for living, but most of all that they will meet the God of the Bible and be forever changed by knowing him.

The Bible Translation Committee
October 2007

A full introduction to the NLT can be found at www.theNLT.com/NLTintro.
A complete list of the translators can be found at www.theNLT.com/scholars.

Psalms

❖ **AUTHORS**
David, Asaph, the sons of Korah, Solomon, Heman, Ethan, and Moses.

❖ **DATE WRITTEN**
Between the time of Moses (about 1440 B.C.) and the Babylonian captivity (586 B.C.).

❖ **PURPOSE**
To provide poetry for the expression of praise, worship, and confession to God.

❖ **THEMES**
Praise, forgiveness, thankfulness, trust, reverence for God and His creation.

Throughout our lives, we experience a wide range of emotions—joy, anger, peacefulness, frustration, despair, happiness, and anxiety. Typically we have trouble sharing these feelings perfectly or completely with others. Yet music and poetry often provide a way to express them fully. The book of Psalms speaks to this part of human experience through the poetic words of people who offered their feelings to God. Are you angry about something? The book of Psalms includes several prayers that express this same emotion (see Psalm 35). Are you afraid? So was David when he wrote Psalm 2. Are you frustrated by injustice? Psalm 79 laments this same situation. Likewise, Psalm 19 and Psalm 104 celebrate the incredible power of God as it is revealed in His creation. This collection of hymns and prayers touches every corner of the human soul. As with the psalm writers themselves, these honest expressions of feeling will draw you closer to the God who made you.

Book One (Psalms 1–41)

1
¹ Oh, the joys of those who do not
    follow the advice of the wicked,
    or stand around with sinners,
    or join in with mockers.
² But they delight in the law of the LORD,
    meditating on it day and night.
³ They are like trees planted along the
    riverbank,
    bearing fruit each season.
Their leaves never wither,
    and they prosper in all they do.

⁴ But not the wicked!
    They are like worthless chaff, scattered
    by the wind.
⁵ They will be condemned at the time of
    judgment.
    Sinners will have no place among the
    godly.
⁶ For the LORD watches over the path of the
    godly,
    but the path of the wicked leads to
    destruction.

2
¹ Why are the nations so angry?
    Why do they waste their time with
    futile plans?
² The kings of the earth prepare for battle;
    the rulers plot together
against the LORD
    and against his anointed one.
³ "Let us break their chains," they cry,
    "and free ourselves from slavery to
    God."

⁴ But the one who rules in heaven laughs.
    The Lord scoffs at them.
⁵ Then in anger he rebukes them,
    terrifying them with his fierce fury.
⁶ For the Lord declares, "I have placed my
    chosen king on the throne
    in Jerusalem,* on my holy
    mountain."

⁷ The king proclaims the LORD's decree:
    "The LORD said to me, 'You are my son.*
    Today I have become your Father.*
⁸ Only ask, and I will give you the nations as
    your inheritance,
    the whole earth as your possession.
⁹ You will break* them with an iron rod
    and smash them like clay pots.'"

¹⁰ Now then, you kings, act wisely!
    Be warned, you rulers of the earth!
¹¹ Serve the LORD with reverent fear,
    and rejoice with trembling.

¹² Submit to God's royal son,* or he will
    become angry,
    and you will be destroyed in the midst
    of all your activities—
for his anger flares up in an instant.
    But what joy for all who take refuge in
    him!

3
*A psalm of David, regarding the time
David fled from his son Absalom.*

¹ O LORD, I have so many enemies;
    so many are against me.
² So many are saying,
    "God will never rescue him!"   *Interlude**

³ But you, O LORD, are a shield around me;
    you are my glory, the one who holds my
    head high.
⁴ I cried out to the LORD,
    and he answered me from his holy
    mountain.   *Interlude*

⁵ I lay down and slept,
    yet I woke up in safety,
    for the LORD was watching over me.
⁶ I am not afraid of ten thousand enemies
    who surround me on every side.

⁷ Arise, O LORD!
    Rescue me, my God!
Slap all my enemies in the face!
    Shatter the teeth of the wicked!
⁸ Victory comes from you, O LORD.
    May you bless your people.   *Interlude*

4
*For the choir director: A psalm of David,
to be accompanied by stringed
instruments.*

¹ Answer me when I call to you,
    O God who declares me innocent.
Free me from my troubles.
    Have mercy on me and hear my prayer.

² How long will you people ruin my
    reputation?
    How long will you make groundless
    accusations?
    How long will you continue your
    lies?   *Interlude*
³ You can be sure of this:
    The LORD set apart the godly for himself.
    The LORD will answer when I call to
    him.

⁴ Don't sin by letting anger control you.
    Think about it overnight and remain
    silent.   *Interlude*

⁵ Offer sacrifices in the right spirit,
  and trust the LORD.

⁶ Many people say, "Who will show us
    better times?"
  Let your face smile on us, LORD.
⁷ You have given me greater joy
    than those who have abundant harvests
    of grain and new wine.
⁸ In peace I will lie down and sleep,
  for you alone, O LORD, will keep me
    safe.

5 For the choir director: A psalm of David,
  to be accompanied by the flute.

¹ O LORD, hear me as I pray;
  pay attention to my groaning.
² Listen to my cry for help, my King and my
    God,
  for I pray to no one but you.
³ Listen to my voice in the morning, LORD.
  Each morning I bring my requests to you
    and wait expectantly.

⁴ O God, you take no pleasure in
    wickedness;
  you cannot tolerate the sins of the
    wicked.
⁵ Therefore, the proud may not stand in
    your presence,
  for you hate all who do evil.
⁶ You will destroy those who tell lies.
  The LORD detests murderers and
    deceivers.

⁷ Because of your unfailing love, I can enter
    your house;
  I will worship at your Temple with
    deepest awe.
⁸ Lead me in the right path, O LORD,
  or my enemies will conquer me.
  Make your way plain for me to follow.

⁹ My enemies cannot speak a truthful word.
  Their deepest desire is to destroy others.
  Their talk is foul, like the stench from an
    open grave.
  Their tongues are filled with flattery.*
¹⁰ O God, declare them guilty.
  Let them be caught in their own traps.
  Drive them away because of their many
    sins,
  for they have rebelled against you.

¹¹ But let all who take refuge in you rejoice;
  let them sing joyful praises forever.
  Spread your protection over them,
    that all who love your name may be
    filled with joy.
¹² For you bless the godly, O LORD;
  you surround them with your shield of
    love.

6 For the choir director: A psalm of David,
  to be accompanied by an eight-stringed
  instrument.*

¹ O LORD, don't rebuke me in your anger
  or discipline me in your rage.
² Have compassion on me, LORD, for I am
    weak.
  Heal me, LORD, for my bones are in
    agony.
³ I am sick at heart.
  How long, O LORD, until you restore me?

⁴ Return, O LORD, and rescue me.
  Save me because of your unfailing love.
⁵ For the dead do not remember you.
  Who can praise you from the grave?*

⁶ I am worn out from sobbing.
  All night I flood my bed with weeping,
    drenching it with my tears.
⁷ My vision is blurred by grief;
  my eyes are worn out because of all my
    enemies.

⁸ Go away, all you who do evil,
  for the LORD has heard my weeping.
⁹ The LORD has heard my plea;
  the LORD will answer my prayer.
¹⁰ May all my enemies be disgraced and
    terrified.
  May they suddenly turn back in
    shame.

7 A psalm of David, which he sang to
  the LORD concerning Cush of the tribe
  of Benjamin.

¹ I come to you for protection, O LORD my
    God.
  Save me from my persecutors—
    rescue me!
² If you don't, they will maul me like a lion,
  tearing me to pieces with no one to
    rescue me.
³ O LORD my God, if I have done wrong
  or am guilty of injustice,
⁴ if I have betrayed a friend
  or plundered my enemy without cause,

2:6 Hebrew on Zion. 2:7a Or Son; also in 2:12. 2:7b Or Today I
reveal you as my son. 2:9 Greek version reads rule. Compare Rev 2:27.
2:12 The meaning of the Hebrew is uncertain. 3:2 Hebrew Selah. The
meaning of this word is uncertain, though it is probably a musical or
literary term. It is rendered Interlude throughout the Psalms. 5:9 Greek
version reads with lies. Compare Rom 3:13. 6:TITLE Hebrew with stringed
instruments; according to the sheminith. 6:5 Hebrew from Sheol?

5 then let my enemies capture me.
    Let them trample me into the ground
    and drag my honor in the dust.

                    Interlude

6 Arise, O LORD, in anger!
    Stand up against the fury of my enemies!
    Wake up, my God, and bring justice!
7 Gather the nations before you.
    Rule over them from on high.
8   The LORD judges the nations.
Declare me righteous, O LORD,
    for I am innocent, O Most High!
9 End the evil of those who are wicked,
    and defend the righteous.
For you look deep within the mind and
    heart,
    O righteous God.

10 God is my shield,
    saving those whose hearts are true and
    right.
11 God is an honest judge.
    He is angry with the wicked every day.

12 If a person does not repent,
    God* will sharpen his sword;
    he will bend and string his bow.
13 He will prepare his deadly weapons
    and shoot his flaming arrows.

14 The wicked conceive evil;
    they are pregnant with trouble
    and give birth to lies.
15 They dig a deep pit to trap others,
    then fall into it themselves.
16 The trouble they make for others backfires
    on them.
    The violence they plan falls on their
    own heads.

17 I will thank the LORD because he is just;
    I will sing praise to the name of the
    LORD Most High.

8 *For the choir director: A psalm of David, to be accompanied by a stringed instrument.**

1 O LORD, our Lord, your majestic name fills
    the earth!
    Your glory is higher than the heavens.
2 You have taught children and infants
    to tell of your strength,*
silencing your enemies
    and all who oppose you.

3 When I look at the night sky and see the
    work of your fingers—
    the moon and the stars you set in place—

4 what are mere mortals that you should
    think about them,
    human beings that you should care for
    them?*
5 Yet you made them only a little lower than
    God*
    and crowned them* with glory and
    honor.
6 You gave them charge of everything you
    made,
    putting all things under their
    authority—
7 the flocks and the herds
    and all the wild animals,
8 the birds in the sky, the fish in the sea,
    and everything that swims the ocean
    currents.

9 O LORD, our Lord, your majestic name fills
    the earth!

9 *For the choir director: A psalm of David, to be sung to the tune "Death of the Son."*

1 I will praise you, LORD, with all my heart;
    I will tell of all the marvelous things you
    have done.
2 I will be filled with joy because of you.
    I will sing praises to your name, O Most
    High.

3 My enemies retreated;
    they staggered and died when you
    appeared.
4 For you have judged in my favor;
    from your throne you have judged with
    fairness.
5 You have rebuked the nations and
    destroyed the wicked;
    you have erased their names forever.
6 The enemy is finished, in endless ruins;
    the cities you uprooted are now
    forgotten.

7 But the LORD reigns forever,
    executing judgment from his throne.
8 He will judge the world with justice
    and rule the nations with fairness.
9 The LORD is a shelter for the oppressed,
    a refuge in times of trouble.
10 Those who know your name trust in you,
    for you, O LORD, do not abandon those
    who search for you.

11 Sing praises to the LORD who reigns in
    Jerusalem.*
    Tell the world about his unforgettable
    deeds.

¹² For he who avenges murder cares for the
   helpless.
   He does not ignore the cries of those
   who suffer.
¹³ LORD, have mercy on me.
   See how my enemies torment me.
   Snatch me back from the jaws of death.
¹⁴ Save me so I can praise you publicly at
   Jerusalem's gates,
   so I can rejoice that you have rescued me.
¹⁵ The nations have fallen into the pit they
   dug for others.
   Their own feet have been caught in the
   trap they set.
¹⁶ The LORD is known for his justice.
   The wicked are trapped by their own
   deeds.   *Quiet Interlude**
¹⁷ The wicked will go down to the grave.*
   This is the fate of all the nations who
   ignore God.
¹⁸ But the needy will not be ignored forever;
   the hopes of the poor will not always be
   crushed.
¹⁹ Arise, O LORD!
   Do not let mere mortals defy you!
   Judge the nations!
²⁰ Make them tremble in fear, O LORD.
   Let the nations know they are merely
   human.   *Interlude*

10 ¹ O LORD, why do you stand so far
         away?
   Why do you hide when I am in trouble?
² The wicked arrogantly hunt down the
   poor.
   Let them be caught in the evil they plan
   for others.
³ For they brag about their evil desires;
   they praise the greedy and curse the
   LORD.
⁴ The wicked are too proud to seek God.
   They seem to think that God is dead.
⁵ Yet they succeed in everything they do.
   They do not see your punishment
   awaiting them.
   They sneer at all their enemies.
⁶ They think, "Nothing bad will ever happen
   to us!
   We will be free of trouble forever!"
⁷ Their mouths are full of cursing, lies, and
   threats.*
   Trouble and evil are on the tips of their
   tongues.

⁸ They lurk in ambush in the villages,
   waiting to murder innocent people.
   They are always searching for helpless
   victims.
⁹ Like lions crouched in hiding,
   they wait to pounce on the helpless.
   Like hunters they capture the helpless
   and drag them away in nets.
¹⁰ Their helpless victims are crushed;
   they fall beneath the strength of the
   wicked.
¹¹ The wicked think, "God isn't
   watching us!
   He has closed his eyes and won't even
   see what we do!"

¹² Arise, O LORD!
   Punish the wicked, O God!
   Do not ignore the helpless!
¹³ Why do the wicked get away with
   despising God?
   They think, "God will never call us to
   account."
¹⁴ But you see the trouble and grief they
   cause.
   You take note of it and punish them.
   The helpless put their trust in you.
   You defend the orphans.
¹⁵ Break the arms of these wicked, evil
   people!
   Go after them until the last one is
   destroyed.
¹⁶ The LORD is king forever and ever!
   The godless nations will vanish from the
   land.
¹⁷ LORD, you know the hopes of the
   helpless.
   Surely you will hear their cries and
   comfort them.
¹⁸ You will bring justice to the orphans and
   the oppressed,
   so mere people can no longer terrify
   them.

11 *For the choir director: A psalm of David.*

¹ I trust in the LORD for protection.
   So why do you say to me,
   "Fly like a bird to the mountains for
   safety!

7:12 Hebrew *he.*   **8:**TITLE Hebrew *according to the gittith.*   **8:2** Greek
version reads *to give you praise.* Compare Matt 21:16.   **8:4** Hebrew *what
is man that you should think of him, / the son of man that you should
care for him?*   **8:5a** Or *Yet you made them only a little lower than the
angels;* Hebrew reads *Yet you made him* [i.e., man] *a little lower than
Elohim.*   **8:5b** Hebrew *him* [i.e., man]; similarly in 8:6.   **9:11** Hebrew
Zion; also in 9:14.   **9:16** Hebrew *Higgaion Selah.* The meaning of this
phrase is uncertain.   **9:17** Hebrew *to Sheol.*   **10:7** Greek version reads
cursing and bitterness. Compare Rom 3:14.

² The wicked are stringing their bows
and fitting their arrows on the
bowstrings.
They shoot from the shadows
at those whose hearts are right.
³ The foundations of law and order have
collapsed.
What can the righteous do?"

⁴ But the LORD is in his holy Temple;
the LORD still rules from heaven.
He watches everyone closely,
examining every person on earth.
⁵ The LORD examines both the righteous
and the wicked.
He hates those who love violence.
⁶ He will rain down blazing coals and
burning sulfur on the wicked,
punishing them with scorching
winds.
⁷ For the righteous LORD loves justice.
The virtuous will see his face.

12 *For the choir director: A psalm
of David, to be accompanied by
an eight-stringed instrument.**

¹ Help, O LORD, for the godly are fast
disappearing!
The faithful have vanished from the
earth!
² Neighbors lie to each other,
speaking with flattering lips and
deceitful hearts.
³ May the LORD cut off their flattering lips
and silence their boastful tongues.
⁴ They say, "We will lie to our hearts'
content.
Our lips are our own—who can
stop us?"

⁵ The LORD replies, "I have seen violence
done to the helpless,
and I have heard the groans of the
poor.
Now I will rise up to rescue them,
as they have longed for me to do."
⁶ The LORD's promises are pure,
like silver refined in a furnace,
purified seven times over.
⁷ Therefore, LORD, we know you will protect
the oppressed,
preserving them forever from this lying
generation,
⁸ even though the wicked strut about,
and evil is praised throughout the
land.

13 *For the choir director: A psalm of David.*

¹ O LORD, how long will you forget me?
Forever?
How long will you look the other way?
² How long must I struggle with anguish in
my soul,
with sorrow in my heart every day?
How long will my enemy have the upper
hand?

³ Turn and answer me, O LORD my God!
Restore the sparkle to my eyes, or I will
die.
⁴ Don't let my enemies gloat, saying, "We
have defeated him!"
Don't let them rejoice at my
downfall.

⁵ But I trust in your unfailing love.
I will rejoice because you have
rescued me.
⁶ I will sing to the LORD
because he is good to me.

14 *For the choir director:
A psalm of David.*

¹ Only fools say in their hearts,
"There is no God."
They are corrupt, and their actions are
evil;
not one of them does good!

² The LORD looks down from heaven
on the entire human race;
he looks to see if anyone is truly wise,
if anyone seeks God.
³ But no, all have turned away;
all have become corrupt.*
No one does good,
not a single one!

⁴ Will those who do evil never learn?
They eat up my people like bread
and wouldn't think of praying to the
LORD.
⁵ Terror will grip them,
for God is with those who obey him.
⁶ The wicked frustrate the plans of the
oppressed,
but the LORD will protect his people.

⁷ Who will come from Mount Zion to rescue
Israel?
When the LORD restores his people,
Jacob will shout with joy, and Israel will
rejoice.

DAY 1

Don't Forget Me, Lord!

D o you ever wonder if the Lord has forgotten you? Does it seem as if He's not paying as much attention to you as He once did? If so, remember that appearances can be deceiving. Regardless of how it looks right now, the Lord is not far from you. He may be giving you an opportunity to trust Him and wait for His help rather than rely on your own resources.

> O LORD, how long will you forget me? Forever? How long will you look the other way?
>
> PSALM 13:1

We are all familiar with a similar kind of testing in everyday life. What parent has not told his child to stay in a certain place until he returns? And what parent is not distressed if that same child is unwilling to wait but quickly runs off on his own?

David, the author of Psalm 13, reflected the thoughts of a child of God who certainly must have pleased the heavenly Father. He was being put to the test. He knew the experience of feeling that he had been abandoned by the Lord. Yet he remained convinced that his only real hope was in God, and that He would reward his faith.

Are you being tested right now? Does God seem far away? It's your opportunity to learn what David learned—that the Lord never leaves you. He sustains all who put their trust in Him. —MRDII

Sometimes, God, even though I know the promises, I cannot find you. When you feel far away, please help me to know that you have not abandoned me. Help me to feel your presence and your love—and help me to keep that relationship strong each day of my life.

He who abandons himself to God
will never be abandoned by God.

DAY 2: pg 12

15 *A psalm of David.*

¹ Who may worship in your sanctuary, LORD?
  Who may enter your presence on your
    holy hill?
² Those who lead blameless lives and do
    what is right,
  speaking the truth from sincere hearts.
³ Those who refuse to gossip
  or harm their neighbors
  or speak evil of their friends.
⁴ Those who despise flagrant sinners,
  and honor the faithful followers of the
    LORD,
  and keep their promises even when it
    hurts.

⁵ Those who lend money without charging
    interest,
  and who cannot be bribed to lie about
    the innocent.
Such people will stand firm forever.

16 *A psalm* of David.*

¹ Keep me safe, O God,
  for I have come to you for refuge.

² I said to the LORD, "You are my Master!
  Every good thing I have comes from
    you."

12:TITLE Hebrew *according to the sheminith.* 14:3 Greek version reads *have become useless.* Compare Rom 3:12. 16:TITLE Hebrew *miktam.* This may be a literary or musical term.

³ The godly people in the land
    are my true heroes!
    I take pleasure in them!
⁴ Troubles multiply for those who chase
        after other gods.
    I will not take part in their sacrifices of
        blood
    or even speak the names of their gods.

⁵ LORD, you alone are my inheritance, my
        cup of blessing.
    You guard all that is mine.
⁶ The land you have given me is a pleasant
        land.
    What a wonderful inheritance!

⁷ I will bless the LORD who guides me;
    even at night my heart instructs me.
⁸ I know the LORD is always with me.
    I will not be shaken, for he is right
        beside me.

⁹ No wonder my heart is glad, and I
        rejoice.*
    My body rests in safety.
¹⁰ For you will not leave my soul among the
        dead*
    or allow your holy one* to rot in the
        grave.
¹¹ You will show me the way of life,
    granting me the joy of your presence
    and the pleasures of living with you
        forever.*

17 *A prayer of David.*

¹ O LORD, hear my plea for justice.
    Listen to my cry for help.
    Pay attention to my prayer,
        for it comes from honest lips.
² Declare me innocent,
    for you see those who do right.

³ You have tested my thoughts and
        examined my heart in the night.
    You have scrutinized me and found
        nothing wrong.
    I am determined not to sin in what
        I say.
⁴ I have followed your commands,
    which keep me from following cruel and
        evil people.
⁵ My steps have stayed on your path;
    I have not wavered from following you.

⁶ I am praying to you because I know you
        will answer, O God.
    Bend down and listen as I pray.

⁷ Show me your unfailing love in wonderful
        ways.
    By your mighty power you rescue
        those who seek refuge from their
        enemies.
⁸ Guard me as you would guard your own
        eyes.*
    Hide me in the shadow of your
        wings.
⁹ Protect me from wicked people who
        attack me,
    from murderous enemies who
        surround me.
¹⁰ They are without pity.
    Listen to their boasting!
¹¹ They track me down and surround me,
    watching for the chance to throw me to
        the ground.
¹² They are like hungry lions, eager to tear
        me apart—
    like young lions hiding in ambush.

¹³ Arise, O LORD!
    Stand against them, and bring them to
        their knees!
    Rescue me from the wicked with your
        sword!
¹⁴ By the power of your hand, O LORD,
    destroy those who look to this world for
        their reward.
    But satisfy the hunger of your treasured
        ones.
    May their children have plenty,
    leaving an inheritance for their
        descendants.
¹⁵ Because I am righteous, I will see you.
    When I awake, I will see you face to face
        and be satisfied.

18 *For the choir director: A psalm of David, the servant of the LORD.*
He sang this song to the LORD on the day the LORD rescued him from all his enemies and from Saul. He sang:

¹ I love you, LORD;
    you are my strength.
² The LORD is my rock, my fortress, and my
        savior;
    my God is my rock, in whom I find
        protection.
    He is my shield, the power that saves me,
        and my place of safety.
³ I called on the LORD, who is worthy of
        praise,
    and he saved me from my enemies.

⁴ The ropes of death entangled me;
  floods of destruction swept over me.
⁵ The grave* wrapped its ropes around me;
  death laid a trap in my path.
⁶ But in my distress I cried out to the LORD;
  yes, I prayed to my God for help.
He heard me from his sanctuary;
  my cry to him reached his ears.

⁷ Then the earth quaked and trembled.
  The foundations of the mountains
    shook;
  they quaked because of his anger.
⁸ Smoke poured from his nostrils;
  fierce flames leaped from his mouth.
  Glowing coals blazed forth from him.
⁹ He opened the heavens and came down;
  dark storm clouds were beneath his feet.
¹⁰ Mounted on a mighty angelic being,* he
    flew,
  soaring on the wings of the wind.
¹¹ He shrouded himself in darkness,
  veiling his approach with dark rain
    clouds.
¹² Thick clouds shielded the brightness
    around him
  and rained down hail and burning
    coals.*
¹³ The LORD thundered from heaven;
  the voice of the Most High resounded
    amid the hail and burning coals.
¹⁴ He shot his arrows and scattered his
    enemies;
  his lightning flashed, and they were
    greatly confused.
¹⁵ Then at your command, O LORD,
  at the blast of your breath,
  the bottom of the sea could be seen,
  and the foundations of the earth were
    laid bare.

¹⁶ He reached down from heaven and
    rescued me;
  he drew me out of deep waters.
¹⁷ He rescued me from my powerful
    enemies,
  from those who hated me and were too
    strong for me.
¹⁸ They attacked me at a moment when I was
    in distress,
  but the LORD supported me.
¹⁹ He led me to a place of safety;
  he rescued me because he delights
    in me.
²⁰ The LORD rewarded me for doing right;
  he restored me because of my
    innocence.

²¹ For I have kept the ways of the LORD;
  I have not turned from my God to follow
    evil.
²² I have followed all his regulations;
  I have never abandoned his decrees.
²³ I am blameless before God;
  I have kept myself from sin.
²⁴ The LORD rewarded me for doing right.
  He has seen my innocence.

²⁵ To the faithful you show yourself faithful;
  to those with integrity you show
    integrity.
²⁶ To the pure you show yourself pure,
  but to the wicked you show yourself
    hostile.
²⁷ You rescue the humble,
  but you humiliate the proud.
²⁸ You light a lamp for me.
  The LORD, my God, lights up my
    darkness.
²⁹ In your strength I can crush an army;
  with my God I can scale any wall.

³⁰ God's way is perfect.
  All the LORD's promises prove true.
  He is a shield for all who look to him for
    protection.
³¹ For who is God except the LORD?
  Who but our God is a solid rock?
³² God arms me with strength,
  and he makes my way perfect.
³³ He makes me as surefooted as a deer,
  enabling me to stand on mountain
    heights.
³⁴ He trains my hands for battle;
  he strengthens my arm to draw a bronze
    bow.
³⁵ You have given me your shield of victory.
  Your right hand supports me;
  your help has made me great.
³⁶ You have made a wide path for my feet
  to keep them from slipping.

³⁷ I chased my enemies and caught them;
  I did not stop until they were conquered.
³⁸ I struck them down so they could not
    get up;
  they fell beneath my feet.
³⁹ You have armed me with strength for the
    battle;
  you have subdued my enemies under
    my feet.

16:9 Greek version reads *and my tongue shouts his praises.*
Compare Acts 2:26. **16:10a** Hebrew *in Sheol.* **16:10b** Or *your Holy*
One. **16:11** Greek version reads *You have shown me the way of life,*
/ and you will fill me with the joy of your presence. Compare Acts
2:28. **17:8** Hebrew *as the pupil of your eye.* **18:5** Hebrew *Sheol.*
18:10 Hebrew *a cherub.* **18:12** Or *and lightning bolts; also in 18:13.*

⁴⁰ You placed my foot on their necks.
   I have destroyed all who hated me.
⁴¹ They called for help, but no one came to
      their rescue.
   They even cried to the LORD, but he
      refused to answer.
⁴² I ground them as fine as dust in the wind.
   I swept them into the gutter like dirt.
⁴³ You gave me victory over my accusers.
   You appointed me ruler over nations;
   people I don't even know now serve me.
⁴⁴ As soon as they hear of me, they submit;
   foreign nations cringe before me.
⁴⁵ They all lose their courage
      and come trembling from their
      strongholds.

⁴⁶ The LORD lives! Praise to my Rock!
   May the God of my salvation be exalted!
⁴⁷ He is the God who pays back those who
      harm me;
   he subdues the nations under me
⁴⁸   and rescues me from my enemies.
   You hold me safe beyond the reach of my
      enemies;
   you save me from violent opponents.
⁴⁹ For this, O LORD, I will praise you among
      the nations;
   I will sing praises to your name.
⁵⁰ You give great victories to your king;
   you show unfailing love to your
      anointed,
   to David and all his descendants forever.

19 *For the choir director:*
      A psalm of David.

¹ The heavens proclaim the glory of God.
   The skies display his craftsmanship.
² Day after day they continue to speak;
   night after night they make him
      known.
³ They speak without a sound or word;
   their voice is never heard.*
⁴ Yet their message has gone throughout the
      earth,
   and their words to all the world.

   God has made a home in the heavens for
      the sun.
⁵ It bursts forth like a radiant bridegroom
      after his wedding.
   It rejoices like a great athlete eager to
      run the race.
⁶ The sun rises at one end of the heavens
   and follows its course to the other end.
   Nothing can hide from its heat.

⁷ The instructions of the LORD are perfect,
   reviving the soul.
   The decrees of the LORD are trustworthy,
   making wise the simple.
⁸ The commandments of the LORD are right,
   bringing joy to the heart.
   The commands of the LORD are clear,
   giving insight for living.
⁹ Reverence for the LORD is pure,
   lasting forever.
   The laws of the LORD are true;
   each one is fair.
¹⁰ They are more desirable than gold,
   even the finest gold.
   They are sweeter than honey,
   even honey dripping from the comb.
¹¹ They are a warning to your servant,
   a great reward for those who obey them.

¹² How can I know all the sins lurking in my
      heart?
   Cleanse me from these hidden faults.
¹³ Keep your servant from deliberate sins!
   Don't let them control me.
   Then I will be free of guilt
   and innocent of great sin.

¹⁴ May the words of my mouth
      and the meditation of my heart
   be pleasing to you,
   O LORD, my rock and my redeemer.

20 *For the choir director:*
      A psalm of David.

¹ In times of trouble, may the LORD answer
      your cry.
   May the name of the God of Jacob keep
      you safe from all harm.
² May he send you help from his sanctuary
   and strengthen you from Jerusalem.*
³ May he remember all your gifts
   and look favorably on your burnt
      offerings.   *Interlude*

⁴ May he grant your heart's desires
   and make all your plans succeed.
⁵ May we shout for joy when we hear of your
      victory
   and raise a victory banner in the name
      of our God.
   May the LORD answer all your prayers.

⁶ Now I know that the LORD rescues his
      anointed king.
   He will answer him from his holy
      heaven
   and rescue him by his great power.

⁷ Some nations boast of their chariots and
horses,
but we boast in the name of the LORD
our God.
⁸ Those nations will fall down and collapse,
but we will rise up and stand firm.

⁹ Give victory to our king, O LORD!
Answer our cry for help.

21 *For the choir director: A psalm of David.*

¹ How the king rejoices in your strength,
O LORD!
He shouts with joy because you give him
victory.
² For you have given him his heart's desire;
you have withheld nothing he
requested.   *Interlude*

³ You welcomed him back with success and
prosperity.
You placed a crown of finest gold on his
head.
⁴ He asked you to preserve his life,
and you granted his request.
The days of his life stretch on forever.
⁵ Your victory brings him great honor,
and you have clothed him with splendor
and majesty.
⁶ You have endowed him with eternal
blessings
and given him the joy of your presence.
⁷ For the king trusts in the LORD.
The unfailing love of the Most High will
keep him from stumbling.

⁸ You will capture all your enemies.
Your strong right hand will seize all who
hate you.
⁹ You will throw them in a flaming furnace
when you appear.
The LORD will consume them in his anger;
fire will devour them.
¹⁰ You will wipe their children from the face
of the earth;
they will never have descendants.
¹¹ Although they plot against you,
their evil schemes will never succeed.
¹² For they will turn and run
when they see your arrows aimed at
them.
¹³ Rise up, O LORD, in all your power.
With music and singing we celebrate
your mighty acts.

22 *For the choir director: A psalm of David, to be sung to the tune "Doe of the Dawn."*

¹ My God, my God, why have you
abandoned me?
Why are you so far away when I groan
for help?
² Every day I call to you, my God, but you do
not answer.
Every night you hear my voice, but I find
no relief.

³ Yet you are holy,
enthroned on the praises of Israel.
⁴ Our ancestors trusted in you,
and you rescued them.
⁵ They cried out to you and were saved.
They trusted in you and were never
disgraced.

⁶ But I am a worm and not a man.
I am scorned and despised by all!
⁷ Everyone who sees me mocks me.
They sneer and shake their heads,
saying,
⁸ "Is this the one who relies on the LORD?
Then let the LORD save him!
If the LORD loves him so much,
let the LORD rescue him!"

⁹ Yet you brought me safely from my
mother's womb
and led me to trust you at my mother's
breast.
¹⁰ I was thrust into your arms at my birth.
You have been my God from the moment
I was born.

¹¹ Do not stay so far from me,
for trouble is near,
and no one else can help me.
¹² My enemies surround me like a herd of
bulls;
fierce bulls of Bashan have hemmed
me in!
¹³ Like lions they open their jaws against me,
roaring and tearing into their prey.
¹⁴ My life is poured out like water,
and all my bones are out of joint.
My heart is like wax,
melting within me.
¹⁵ My strength has dried up like sunbaked
clay.
My tongue sticks to the roof of my mouth.
You have laid me in the dust and left me
for dead.

19:3 Or *There is no speech or language where their voice is not heard.*
20:2 Hebrew *Zion.*

DAY 2

Divine Revelation

Some people believe that the Bible is merely a haphazard collection of ancient writings. But we have good reason to believe it is God's inspired Word. For example, the Bible contains prophecies that have been fulfilled.

Centuries before specific events took place, the writers of Scripture predicted their occurrence, and in the course of time those events came to pass.

> *My enemies surround me like a pack of dogs; an evil gang closes in on me. They have pierced my hands and feet. . . . They divide my garments among themselves and throw dice for my clothing.*
>
> PSALM 22:16–18

No matter how farsighted we may be, we cannot foretell the future with any precision. Indeed, our best guesses often turn out to be wrong. Here are some examples:

"Airplanes are interesting toys but of no military value." Who said that? A renowned professor of military strategy. "Stocks have reached what looks like a permanently high plateau." This pronouncement was made by a distinguished economist just before the financial crash of 1929.

The Bible, however, is filled with dramatic examples of fulfilled prophecy. Isaiah 52:13–53:12 and Psalm 22:1–18 record details about the crucifixion of Christ hundreds of years before this cruel form of execution was ever practiced.

When we pick up the Bible, we can rest assured that we are holding in our hands the one authoritative divine revelation of truth—a claim verified by fulfilled prophecy. —VCG

Dear Lord, we are so grateful that the Bible is true. We see this in fulfilled prophecy and in changed lives. Continue to use your inspired Word to guide, correct, and instruct us.

You can trust the Bible—God always keeps His word.

DAY 3: pg 14

16 My enemies surround me like a pack of dogs;
   an evil gang closes in on me.
   They have pierced my hands and feet.
17 I can count all my bones.
   My enemies stare at me and gloat.
18 They divide my garments among themselves
   and throw dice* for my clothing.

19 O LORD, do not stay far away!
   You are my strength; come quickly to my aid!
20 Save me from the sword;
   spare my precious life from these dogs.

21 Snatch me from the lion's jaws
   and from the horns of these wild oxen.
22 I will proclaim your name to my brothers and sisters.*
   I will praise you among your assembled people.
23 Praise the LORD, all you who fear him!
   Honor him, all you descendants of Jacob!
   Show him reverence, all you descendants of Israel!
24 For he has not ignored or belittled the suffering of the needy.
   He has not turned his back on them,
   but has listened to their cries for help.

²⁵ I will praise you in the great assembly.
I will fulfill my vows in the presence of
those who worship you.
²⁶ The poor will eat and be satisfied.
All who seek the LORD will praise him.
Their hearts will rejoice with everlasting
joy.
²⁷ The whole earth will acknowledge the
LORD and return to him.
All the families of the nations will bow
down before him.
²⁸ For royal power belongs to the LORD.
He rules all the nations.

²⁹ Let the rich of the earth feast and worship.
Bow before him, all who are mortal,
all whose lives will end as dust.
³⁰ Our children will also serve him.
Future generations will hear about the
wonders of the Lord.
³¹ His righteous acts will be told to those not
yet born.
They will hear about everything he has
done.

23 *A psalm of David.*

¹ The LORD is my shepherd;
I have all that I need.
² He lets me rest in green meadows;
he leads me beside peaceful streams.
³ He renews my strength.
He guides me along right paths,
bringing honor to his name.
⁴ Even when I walk
through the darkest valley,*
I will not be afraid,
for you are close beside me.
Your rod and your staff
protect and comfort me.
⁵ You prepare a feast for me
in the presence of my enemies.
You honor me by anointing my head with
oil.
My cup overflows with blessings.
⁶ Surely your goodness and unfailing love
will pursue me
all the days of my life,
and I will live in the house of the LORD
forever.

24 *A psalm of David.*

¹ The earth is the LORD's, and everything
in it.
The world and all its people belong to
him.

² For he laid the earth's foundation on the
seas
and built it on the ocean depths.

³ Who may climb the mountain of the LORD?
Who may stand in his holy place?
⁴ Only those whose hands and hearts are
pure,
who do not worship idols
and never tell lies.
⁵ They will receive the LORD's blessing
and have a right relationship with God
their savior.
⁶ Such people may seek you
and worship in your presence, O God of
Jacob.   *Interlude*

⁷ Open up, ancient gates!
Open up, ancient doors,
and let the King of glory enter.
⁸ Who is the King of glory?
The LORD, strong and mighty;
the LORD, invincible in battle.
⁹ Open up, ancient gates!
Open up, ancient doors,
and let the King of glory enter.
¹⁰ Who is the King of glory?
The LORD of Heaven's Armies—
he is the King of glory.   *Interlude*

25 * *A psalm of David.*

¹ O LORD, I give my life to you.
²   I trust in you, my God!
Do not let me be disgraced,
or let my enemies rejoice in my defeat.
³ No one who trusts in you will ever be
disgraced,
but disgrace comes to those who try to
deceive others.

⁴ Show me the right path, O LORD;
point out the road for me to follow.
⁵ Lead me by your truth and teach me,
for you are the God who saves me.
All day long I put my hope in you.
⁶ Remember, O LORD, your compassion and
unfailing love,
which you have shown from long ages
past.
⁷ Do not remember the rebellious sins of my
youth.
Remember me in the light of your
unfailing love,
for you are merciful, O LORD.

22:18 Hebrew *cast lots.* **22:22** Hebrew *my brothers.* **23:4** Or *the dark
valley of death.* **25** This psalm is a Hebrew acrostic poem; each verse
begins with a successive letter of the Hebrew alphabet.

Renewed Strength

OUR DAILY BREAD PSALM 23

I n his classic book *A Shepherd Looks at Psalm 23*, W. Phillip Keller gives a striking picture of the care and gentleness of a shepherd. In verse 3 when David says, "He renews my strength," he uses language every shepherd would understand.

Sheep are built in such a way that if they fall over on their side and then onto their back, it is very difficult for them to get up again. They flail their legs in the air, bleat, and cry. After a few hours on their backs, gas begins to collect in their stomachs, the stomach hardens, the air passage is cut off, and the sheep will eventually suffocate. This is referred to as a "cast down" position.

When a shepherd restores a cast down sheep, he reassures it, massages its legs to restore circulation, gently turns the sheep over, lifts it up, and holds it so it can regain its equilibrium.

What a picture of what God wants to do for us! When we are on our backs, flailing because of guilt, grief, or grudges, our loving Shepherd renews us with His grace, lifts us up, and holds us until we've gained our spiritual equilibrium.

If you've been cast down for any reason, God is the only one who can help you get on your feet again. He will restore your confidence, joy, and strength. —MLW

> The LORD is my shepherd; I have all that I need.... He renews my strength. He guides me along right paths, bringing honor to his name.
>
> PSALM 23:1–3

Lord, when I feel helpless and hopeless, please be my comforting shepherd. Please lift me up, give me strength, and assure me that you will guide me and support me the next time I feel as if I cannot go on alone. Thank you for being my shepherd.

The weak and the helpless are in the Good Shepherd's special care.

DAY 4: pg 17

8 The LORD is good and does what is right;
   he shows the proper path to those who
   go astray.
9 He leads the humble in doing right,
   teaching them his way.
10 The LORD leads with unfailing love and
   faithfulness
   all who keep his covenant and obey his
   demands.
11 For the honor of your name, O LORD,
   forgive my many, many sins.
12 Who are those who fear the LORD?
   He will show them the path they should
   choose.

13 They will live in prosperity,
   and their children will inherit the land.
14 The LORD is a friend to those who fear
   him.
   He teaches them his covenant.
15 My eyes are always on the LORD,
   for he rescues me from the traps of my
   enemies.
16 Turn to me and have mercy,
   for I am alone and in deep distress.
17 My problems go from bad to worse.
   Oh, save me from them all!
18 Feel my pain and see my trouble.
   Forgive all my sins.

¹⁹ See how many enemies I have
　　and how viciously they hate me!
²⁰ Protect me! Rescue my life from them!
　　Do not let me be disgraced, for in you I
　　　　take refuge.
²¹ May integrity and honesty protect me,
　　for I put my hope in you.

²² O God, ransom Israel
　　from all its troubles.

26 *A psalm of David.*

¹ Declare me innocent, O LORD,
　　for I have acted with integrity;
　　I have trusted in the LORD without
　　　　wavering.
² Put me on trial, LORD, and cross-
　　　　examine me.
　　Test my motives and my heart.
³ For I am always aware of your unfailing
　　　　love,
　　and I have lived according to your truth.
⁴ I do not spend time with liars
　　or go along with hypocrites.
⁵ I hate the gatherings of those who do evil,
　　and I refuse to join in with the wicked.
⁶ I wash my hands to declare my
　　　　innocence.
　　I come to your altar, O LORD,
⁷ singing a song of thanksgiving
　　and telling of all your wonders.
⁸ I love your sanctuary, LORD,
　　the place where your glorious presence
　　　　dwells.

⁹ Don't let me suffer the fate of sinners.
　　Don't condemn me along with
　　　　murderers.
¹⁰ Their hands are dirty with evil schemes,
　　and they constantly take bribes.
¹¹ But I am not like that; I live with integrity.
　　So redeem me and show me mercy.
¹² Now I stand on solid ground,
　　and I will publicly praise the LORD.

27 *A psalm of David.*

¹ The LORD is my light and my salvation—
　　so why should I be afraid?
　　The LORD is my fortress, protecting me
　　　　from danger,
　　so why should I tremble?
² When evil people come to devour me,
　　when my enemies and foes attack me,
　　they will stumble and fall.

³ Though a mighty army surrounds me,
　　my heart will not be afraid.
　　Even if I am attacked,
　　I will remain confident.
⁴ The one thing I ask of the LORD—
　　the thing I seek most—
　　is to live in the house of the LORD all the
　　　　days of my life,
　　delighting in the LORD's perfections
　　and meditating in his Temple.
⁵ For he will conceal me there when
　　　　troubles come;
　　he will hide me in his sanctuary.
　　He will place me out of reach on a high
　　　　rock.
⁶ Then I will hold my head high
　　above my enemies who surround me.
　　At his sanctuary I will offer sacrifices with
　　　　shouts of joy,
　　singing and praising the LORD with music.

⁷ Hear me as I pray, O LORD.
　　Be merciful and answer me!
⁸ My heart has heard you say, "Come and
　　　　talk with me."
　　And my heart responds, "LORD, I am
　　　　coming."
⁹ Do not turn your back on me.
　　Do not reject your servant in anger.
　　You have always been my helper.
　　Don't leave me now; don't abandon me,
　　O God of my salvation!
¹⁰ Even if my father and mother abandon me,
　　the LORD will hold me close.

¹¹ Teach me how to live, O LORD.
　　Lead me along the right path,
　　for my enemies are waiting for me.
¹² Do not let me fall into their hands.
　　For they accuse me of things I've never
　　　　done;
　　with every breath they threaten me with
　　　　violence.
¹³ Yet I am confident I will see the LORD's
　　　　goodness
　　while I am here in the land of the living.

¹⁴ Wait patiently for the LORD.
　　Be brave and courageous.
　　Yes, wait patiently for the LORD.

28 *A psalm of David.*

¹ I pray to you, O LORD, my rock.
　　Do not turn a deaf ear to me.
　　For if you are silent,
　　I might as well give up and die.

2 Listen to my prayer for mercy
as I cry out to you for help,
as I lift my hands toward your holy
sanctuary.

3 Do not drag me away with the wicked—
with those who do evil—
those who speak friendly words to their
neighbors
while planning evil in their hearts.
4 Give them the punishment they so richly
deserve!
Measure it out in proportion to their
wickedness.
Pay them back for all their evil deeds!
Give them a taste of what they have
done to others.
5 They care nothing for what the LORD has
done
or for what his hands have made.
So he will tear them down,
and they will never be rebuilt!

6 Praise the LORD!
For he has heard my cry for mercy.
7 The LORD is my strength and shield.
I trust him with all my heart.
He helps me, and my heart is filled with
joy.
I burst out in songs of thanksgiving.

8 The LORD gives his people strength.
He is a safe fortress for his anointed king.
9 Save your people!
Bless Israel, your special possession.*
Lead them like a shepherd,
and carry them in your arms forever.

29 A psalm of David.

1 Honor the LORD, you heavenly beings*;
honor the LORD for his glory and
strength.
2 Honor the LORD for the glory of his name.
Worship the LORD in the splendor of his
holiness.

3 The voice of the LORD echoes above the
sea.
The God of glory thunders.
The LORD thunders over the mighty sea.
4 The voice of the LORD is powerful;
the voice of the LORD is majestic.
5 The voice of the LORD splits the mighty
cedars;
the LORD shatters the cedars of
Lebanon.

6 He makes Lebanon's mountains skip like a
calf;
he makes Mount Hermon* leap like a
young wild ox.
7 The voice of the LORD strikes
with bolts of lightning.
8 The voice of the LORD makes the barren
wilderness quake;
the LORD shakes the wilderness of
Kadesh.
9 The voice of the LORD twists mighty oaks*
and strips the forests bare.
In his Temple everyone shouts, "Glory!"

10 The LORD rules over the floodwaters.
The LORD reigns as king forever.
11 The LORD gives his people strength.
The LORD blesses them with peace.

30 A psalm of David. A song for the dedication of the Temple.

1 I will exalt you, LORD, for you rescued me.
You refused to let my enemies triumph
over me.
2 O LORD my God, I cried to you for help,
and you restored my health.
3 You brought me up from the grave,*
O LORD.
You kept me from falling into the pit of
death.

4 Sing to the LORD, all you godly ones!
Praise his holy name.
5 For his anger lasts only a moment,
but his favor lasts a lifetime!
Weeping may last through the night,
but joy comes with the morning.

6 When I was prosperous, I said,
"Nothing can stop me now!"
7 Your favor, O LORD, made me as secure as
a mountain.
Then you turned away from me, and I
was shattered.

8 I cried out to you, O LORD.
I begged the Lord for mercy, saying,
9 "What will you gain if I die,
if I sink into the grave?
Can my dust praise you?
Can it tell of your faithfulness?
10 Hear me, LORD, and have mercy on me.
Help me, O LORD."

11 You have turned my mourning into joyful
dancing.
You have taken away my clothes of
mourning and clothed me with joy,

Time to Praise

DAY 4

OUR DAILY BREAD PSALM 30

I t was the worst of times. In the first half of the seventeenth century, Germany was in the midst of wars and famine and pestilence. In the city of Eilenburg lived a pastor by the name of Martin Rinkart.

During one especially oppressive period, Rinkart conducted up to fifty funerals a day as a plague swept through the town and as the Thirty Years' War wreaked its own terror on the people. Among those whom Rinkart buried were members of his own family.

Yet during those years of darkness and despair, when death and destruction greeted each new day, Pastor Rinkart wrote sixty-six sacred songs and hymns. Among them was the song "Now Thank We All Our God." As sorrow crouched all around him, Rinkart wrote:

> Now thank we all our God
> With hearts and hands and voices,
> Who wondrous things hath done,
> In whom His world rejoices;
> Who, from our mothers' arms,
> Hath blessed us on our way
> With countless gifts of love,
> And still is ours today.

Rinkart demonstrated a valuable lesson for us all: Thankfulness does not have to wait for prosperity and peace. It's always a good time to praise God for the "wondrous things" He has done. —JDB

In the darkest of times, Father, you are with me. What wondrous gifts you give each day! I praise you and thank you for your presence and for your grace in times of sorrow.

> You have turned my mourning into joyful dancing. You have taken away my clothes of mourning and clothed me with joy, that I might sing praises to you and not be silent.
>
> PSALM 30:11–12

A heart in tune with God can sing praises even in the darkest night.

DAY 5: pg 19

---

¹² that I might sing praises to you and not be silent.
O LORD my God, I will give you thanks forever!

31 *For the choir director: A psalm of David.*

¹ O LORD, I have come to you for protection; don't let me be disgraced. Save me, for you do what is right.

² Turn your ear to listen to me; rescue me quickly. Be my rock of protection, a fortress where I will be safe.
³ You are my rock and my fortress. For the honor of your name, lead me out of this danger.

28:9 Hebrew *Bless your inheritance.* 29:1 Hebrew *you sons of God.*
29:6 Hebrew *Sirion,* another name for Mount Hermon. 29:9 Or *causes the deer to writhe in labor.* 30:3 Hebrew *from Sheol.*

⁴ Pull me from the trap my enemies set
for me,
for I find protection in you alone.
⁵ I entrust my spirit into your hand.
Rescue me, LORD, for you are a faithful
God.

⁶ I hate those who worship worthless idols.
I trust in the LORD.
⁷ I will be glad and rejoice in your unfailing
love,
for you have seen my troubles,
and you care about the anguish of my
soul.
⁸ You have not handed me over to my
enemies
but have set me in a safe place.

⁹ Have mercy on me, LORD, for I am in distress.
Tears blur my eyes.
My body and soul are withering away.
¹⁰ I am dying from grief;
my years are shortened by sadness.
Sin has drained my strength;
I am wasting away from within.
¹¹ I am scorned by all my enemies
and despised by my neighbors—
even my friends are afraid to come
near me.
When they see me on the street,
they run the other way.
¹² I am ignored as if I were dead,
as if I were a broken pot.
¹³ I have heard the many rumors about me,
and I am surrounded by terror.
My enemies conspire against me,
plotting to take my life.

¹⁴ But I am trusting you, O LORD,
saying, "You are my God!"
¹⁵ My future is in your hands.
Rescue me from those who hunt me
down relentlessly.
¹⁶ Let your favor shine on your servant.
In your unfailing love, rescue me.
¹⁷ Don't let me be disgraced, O LORD,
for I call out to you for help.
Let the wicked be disgraced;
let them lie silent in the grave.*
¹⁸ Silence their lying lips—
those proud and arrogant lips that
accuse the godly.

¹⁹ How great is the goodness
you have stored up for those who fear
you.
You lavish it on those who come to you for
protection,
blessing them before the watching world.

²⁰ You hide them in the shelter of your
presence,
safe from those who conspire against
them.
You shelter them in your presence,
far from accusing tongues.

²¹ Praise the LORD,
for he has shown me the wonders of his
unfailing love.
He kept me safe when my city was
under attack.
²² In panic I cried out,
"I am cut off from the LORD!"
But you heard my cry for mercy
and answered my call for help.

²³ Love the LORD, all you godly ones!
For the LORD protects those who are
loyal to him,
but he harshly punishes the arrogant.
²⁴ So be strong and courageous,
all you who put your hope in the
LORD!

32 *A psalm* of David.*

¹ Oh, what joy for those
whose disobedience is forgiven,
whose sin is put out of sight!
² Yes, what joy for those
whose record the LORD has cleared of
guilt,*
whose lives are lived in complete
honesty!
³ When I refused to confess my sin,
my body wasted away,
and I groaned all day long.
⁴ Day and night your hand of discipline was
heavy on me.
My strength evaporated like water in the
summer heat.   *Interlude*

⁵ Finally, I confessed all my sins to you
and stopped trying to hide my guilt.
I said to myself, "I will confess my
rebellion to the LORD."
And you forgave me! All my guilt is
gone.   *Interlude*

⁶ Therefore, let all the godly pray to you
while there is still time,
that they may not drown in the
floodwaters of judgment.
⁷ For you are my hiding place;
you protect me from trouble.
You surround me with songs of victory.
                    Interlude

Instincts

OUR DAILY BREAD PSALM 32

F lying into a storm is a dangerous experience. The temptation is to fly by your instincts, or, as aviators say, "by the seat of your pants." But as any pilot will tell you, that's a prescription for disaster. If you rely on your feelings and instincts, you become disoriented, thinking the plane is going up when it's actually going down. Thankfully, the instrument panel is set to magnetic north and can be trusted every time. Letting your instruments guide you, even when it feels like they're wrong, helps ensure safety in the storm.

We all face storms that threaten to confuse and disorient us. It may be a call from the doctor's office, a friend who has betrayed us, or a shattered dream. Those are the times to be especially careful. When you are blinded by life's disappointments, don't trust your instincts. Flying by the seat of your pants in the storms of life can lead to despair, confusion, and vengeful responses that make matters worse. God wants to guide you, and His Word is packed with wisdom and insights for living. His "word is a lamp to guide my feet and a light for my path" (Ps 119:105). Where He leads is always right!

Go to your Bible, and trust God to guide you. He promises, "I will guide you along the best pathway for your life" (32:8). —JMS

> **I will guide you along the best pathway for your life. I will advise you and watch over you.**
>
> PSALM 32:8

Dear God, I'm so glad I don't have to rely on my instincts to get by in this life! You've given me the ultimate guidebook, the Bible. Help me to walk in its light.

The closer we walk with God, the clearer we see His guidance.

DAY 6: pg 23

⁸ The LORD says, "I will guide you along the
    best pathway for your life.
  I will advise you and watch over you.
⁹ Do not be like a senseless horse or
    mule
  that needs a bit and bridle to keep it
    under control."

¹⁰ Many sorrows come to the wicked,
  but unfailing love surrounds those who
    trust the LORD.
¹¹ So rejoice in the LORD and be glad, all you
    who obey him!
  Shout for joy, all you whose hearts are
    pure!

33 ¹ Let the godly sing for joy to the
    LORD;
  it is fitting for the pure to praise him.
² Praise the LORD with melodies on the lyre;
  make music for him on the ten-stringed
    harp.
³ Sing a new song of praise to him;
  play skillfully on the harp, and sing
    with joy.
⁴ For the word of the LORD holds true,
  and we can trust everything he does.
⁵ He loves whatever is just and good;
  the unfailing love of the LORD fills the
    earth.

31:17 Hebrew *in Sheol.* **32:TITLE** Hebrew *maskil.* This may be a literary or musical term. **32:2** Greek version reads *of sin.* Compare Rom 4:7.

⁶ The LORD merely spoke,
    and the heavens were created.
He breathed the word,
    and all the stars were born.
⁷ He assigned the sea its boundaries
    and locked the oceans in vast
        reservoirs.
⁸ Let the whole world fear the LORD,
    and let everyone stand in awe of him.
⁹ For when he spoke, the world began!
    It appeared at his command.

¹⁰ The LORD frustrates the plans of the nations
    and thwarts all their schemes.
¹¹ But the LORD's plans stand firm forever;
    his intentions can never be shaken.

¹² What joy for the nation whose God is the
    LORD,
    whose people he has chosen as his
        inheritance.

¹³ The LORD looks down from heaven
    and sees the whole human race.
¹⁴ From his throne he observes
    all who live on the earth.
¹⁵ He made their hearts,
    so he understands everything they do.
¹⁶ The best-equipped army cannot save a
    king,
    nor is great strength enough to save a
        warrior.
¹⁷ Don't count on your warhorse to give you
    victory—
    for all its strength, it cannot save you.

¹⁸ But the LORD watches over those who fear
    him,
    those who rely on his unfailing love.
¹⁹ He rescues them from death
    and keeps them alive in times of famine.

²⁰ We put our hope in the LORD.
    He is our help and our shield.
²¹ In him our hearts rejoice,
    for we trust in his holy name.
²² Let your unfailing love surround us, LORD,
    for our hope is in you alone.

34 * A psalm of David, regarding the time he pretended to be insane in front of Abimelech, who sent him away.

¹ I will praise the LORD at all times.
    I will constantly speak his praises.
² I will boast only in the LORD;
    let all who are helpless take heart.
³ Come, let us tell of the LORD's greatness;
    let us exalt his name together.

⁴ I prayed to the LORD, and he answered me.
    He freed me from all my fears.
⁵ Those who look to him for help will be
    radiant with joy;
    no shadow of shame will darken their
        faces.
⁶ In my desperation I prayed, and the LORD
    listened;
    he saved me from all my troubles.
⁷ For the angel of the LORD is a guard;
    he surrounds and defends all who fear
        him.

⁸ Taste and see that the LORD is good.
    Oh, the joys of those who take refuge in
        him!
⁹ Fear the LORD, you his godly people,
    for those who fear him will have all they
        need.
¹⁰ Even strong young lions sometimes go
    hungry,
    but those who trust in the LORD will lack
        no good thing.

¹¹ Come, my children, and listen to me,
    and I will teach you to fear the LORD.
¹² Does anyone want to live a life
    that is long and prosperous?
¹³ Then keep your tongue from speaking evil
    and your lips from telling lies!
¹⁴ Turn away from evil and do good.
    Search for peace, and work to
        maintain it.

¹⁵ The eyes of the LORD watch over those
    who do right;
    his ears are open to their cries for help.
¹⁶ But the LORD turns his face against those
    who do evil;
    he will erase their memory from the
        earth.
¹⁷ The LORD hears his people when they call
    to him for help.
    He rescues them from all their troubles.
¹⁸ The LORD is close to the brokenhearted;
    he rescues those whose spirits are
        crushed.

¹⁹ The righteous person faces many troubles,
    but the LORD comes to the rescue each
        time.
²⁰ For the LORD protects the bones of the
    righteous;
    not one of them is broken!

²¹ Calamity will surely overtake the wicked,
    and those who hate the righteous will
        be punished.

²² But the LORD will redeem those who serve him.
No one who takes refuge in him will be condemned.

35 *A psalm of David.*

¹ O LORD, oppose those who oppose me.
Fight those who fight against me.
² Put on your armor, and take up your shield.
Prepare for battle, and come to my aid.
³ Lift up your spear and javelin
against those who pursue me.
Let me hear you say,
"I will give you victory!"
⁴ Bring shame and disgrace on those trying to kill me;
turn them back and humiliate those who want to harm me.
⁵ Blow them away like chaff in the wind—
a wind sent by the angel of the LORD.
⁶ Make their path dark and slippery,
with the angel of the LORD pursuing them.
⁷ I did them no wrong, but they laid a trap for me.
I did them no wrong, but they dug a pit to catch me.
⁸ So let sudden ruin come upon them!
Let them be caught in the trap they set for me!
Let them be destroyed in the pit they dug for me.

⁹ Then I will rejoice in the LORD.
I will be glad because he rescues me.
¹⁰ With every bone in my body I will praise him:
"LORD, who can compare with you?
Who else rescues the helpless from the strong?
Who else protects the helpless and poor from those who rob them?"

¹¹ Malicious witnesses testify against me.
They accuse me of crimes I know nothing about.
¹² They repay me evil for good.
I am sick with despair.
¹³ Yet when they were ill, I grieved for them.
I denied myself by fasting for them,
but my prayers returned unanswered.
¹⁴ I was sad, as though they were my friends or family,
as if I were grieving for my own mother.

¹⁵ But they are glad now that I am in trouble;
they gleefully join together against me.
I am attacked by people I don't even know;
they slander me constantly.
¹⁶ They mock me and call me names;
they snarl at me.

¹⁷ How long, O Lord, will you look on and do nothing?
Rescue me from their fierce attacks.
Protect my life from these lions!
¹⁸ Then I will thank you in front of the great assembly.
I will praise you before all the people.
¹⁹ Don't let my treacherous enemies rejoice over my defeat.
Don't let those who hate me without cause gloat over my sorrow.
²⁰ They don't talk of peace;
they plot against innocent people who mind their own business.
²¹ They shout, "Aha! Aha!
With our own eyes we saw him do it!"

²² O LORD, you know all about this.
Do not stay silent.
Do not abandon me now, O Lord.
²³ Wake up! Rise to my defense!
Take up my case, my God and my Lord.
²⁴ Declare me not guilty, O LORD my God, for you give justice.
Don't let my enemies laugh about me in my troubles.
²⁵ Don't let them say, "Look, we got what we wanted!
Now we will eat him alive!"

²⁶ May those who rejoice at my troubles
be humiliated and disgraced.
May those who triumph over me
be covered with shame and dishonor.
²⁷ But give great joy to those who came to my defense.
Let them continually say, "Great is the LORD,
who delights in blessing his servant with peace!"
²⁸ Then I will proclaim your justice,
and I will praise you all day long.

36 *For the choir director: A psalm of David, the servant of the LORD.*

¹ Sin whispers to the wicked, deep within their hearts.
They have no fear of God at all.

34 This psalm is a Hebrew acrostic poem; each verse begins with a successive letter of the Hebrew alphabet.

2 In their blind conceit,
    they cannot see how wicked they really
    are.
3 Everything they say is crooked and
    deceitful.
    They refuse to act wisely or do good.
4 They lie awake at night, hatching sinful
    plots.
    Their actions are never good.
    They make no attempt to turn from
    evil.

5 Your unfailing love, O Lord, is as vast as
    the heavens;
    your faithfulness reaches beyond the
    clouds.
6 Your righteousness is like the mighty
    mountains,
    your justice like the ocean depths.
    You care for people and animals alike,
    O Lord.
7   How precious is your unfailing love,
    O God!
    All humanity finds shelter
    in the shadow of your wings.
8 You feed them from the abundance of your
    own house,
    letting them drink from your river of
    delights.
9 For you are the fountain of life,
    the light by which we see.

10 Pour out your unfailing love on those who
    love you;
    give justice to those with honest
    hearts.
11 Don't let the proud trample me
    or the wicked push me around.
12 Look! Those who do evil have fallen!
    They are thrown down, never to rise
    again.

37 * A psalm of David.

1 Don't worry about the wicked
    or envy those who do wrong.
2 For like grass, they soon fade away.
    Like spring flowers, they soon wither.

3 Trust in the Lord and do good.
    Then you will live safely in the land and
    prosper.
4 Take delight in the Lord,
    and he will give you your heart's
    desires.

5 Commit everything you do to the Lord.
    Trust him, and he will help you.

6 He will make your innocence radiate like
    the dawn,
    and the justice of your cause will shine
    like the noonday sun.

7 Be still in the presence of the Lord,
    and wait patiently for him to act.
    Don't worry about evil people who
    prosper
    or fret about their wicked schemes.

8 Stop being angry!
    Turn from your rage!
    Do not lose your temper—
    it only leads to harm.
9 For the wicked will be destroyed,
    but those who trust in the Lord will
    possess the land.

10 Soon the wicked will disappear.
    Though you look for them, they will be
    gone.
11 The lowly will possess the land
    and will live in peace and prosperity.

12 The wicked plot against the godly;
    they snarl at them in defiance.
13 But the Lord just laughs,
    for he sees their day of judgment
    coming.

14 The wicked draw their swords
    and string their bows
    to kill the poor and the oppressed,
    to slaughter those who do right.
15 But their swords will stab their own
    hearts,
    and their bows will be broken.

16 It is better to be godly and have little
    than to be evil and rich.
17 For the strength of the wicked will be
    shattered,
    but the Lord takes care of the godly.

18 Day by day the Lord takes care of the
    innocent,
    and they will receive an inheritance that
    lasts forever.
19 They will not be disgraced in hard times;
    even in famine they will have more than
    enough.

20 But the wicked will die.
    The Lord's enemies are like flowers in
    a field—
    they will disappear like smoke.

21 The wicked borrow and never repay,
    but the godly are generous givers.

Feelings and Faithfulness

DAY 6

OUR DAILY BREAD PSALM 36

When I was in college, my roommate was engaged to a woman who lived eight hundred miles away. He was a worrier and a pessimist, so he was constantly questioning the closeness of their relationship. He would worry that they were drifting apart. If a day came without a letter, he would convince himself that she didn't love him any longer and was about to break up with him.

I would get so fed up with his worrying that I would insist he call her. He always discovered that nothing had changed and that she was not wavering in her love. Greatly relieved, he would kick himself for having doubted, and he would promise not to worry again—which lasted about three days!

Although we sometimes falter in our faith and question God's love for us, He remains faithful. Even when we doubt His promises, or don't feel close to Him, or choose to sin, His faithfulness still "reaches beyond the clouds" (Ps 36:5). We can be sure God will do all He said He would do (1 Thes 5:24; 2 Thes 3:3). His promises are backed up by His flawless character.

In those times when you don't feel close to God, remind yourself that His feelings for you haven't changed. It's not a matter of how you feel at the moment, but the fact of the rock-solid faithfulness of God. —DCE

> **Your unfailing love, O LORD, is as vast as the heavens; your faithfulness reaches beyond the clouds.**
>
> PSALM 36:5

I admit, Lord, that many times I experience fear, doubt, and worry. Thank you that because of your unchanging faithfulness and love I can stand on solid ground and not allow these emotions to overwhelm me.

Trusting God's faithfulness dispels our fearfulness.

DAY 7: pg 25

²² Those the LORD blesses will possess the land,
but those he curses will die.

²³ The LORD directs the steps of the godly.
He delights in every detail of their lives.
²⁴ Though they stumble, they will never fall,
for the LORD holds them by the hand.

²⁵ Once I was young, and now I am old.
Yet I have never seen the godly abandoned
or their children begging for bread.
²⁶ The godly always give generous loans to others,
and their children are a blessing.

²⁷ Turn from evil and do good,
and you will live in the land forever.
²⁸ For the LORD loves justice,
and he will never abandon the godly.

He will keep them safe forever,
but the children of the wicked will die.
²⁹ The godly will possess the land
and will live there forever.

³⁰ The godly offer good counsel;
they teach right from wrong.
³¹ They have made God's law their own,
so they will never slip from his path.

37 This psalm is a Hebrew acrostic poem; each stanza begins with a successive letter of the Hebrew alphabet.

³² The wicked wait in ambush for the godly,
  looking for an excuse to kill them.
³³ But the LORD will not let the wicked succeed
  or let the godly be condemned when
  they are put on trial.

³⁴ Put your hope in the LORD.
  Travel steadily along his path.
  He will honor you by giving you the land.
  You will see the wicked destroyed.

³⁵ I have seen wicked and ruthless people
  flourishing like a tree in its native soil.
³⁶ But when I looked again, they were gone!
  Though I searched for them, I could not
  find them!

³⁷ Look at those who are honest and good,
  for a wonderful future awaits those who
  love peace.
³⁸ But the rebellious will be destroyed;
  they have no future.

³⁹ The LORD rescues the godly;
  he is their fortress in times of trouble.
⁴⁰ The LORD helps them,
  rescuing them from the wicked.
  He saves them,
  and they find shelter in him.

38

*A psalm of David, asking God
to remember him.*

¹ O LORD, don't rebuke me in your anger
  or discipline me in your rage!
² Your arrows have struck deep,
  and your blows are crushing me.
³ Because of your anger, my whole body is
  sick;
  my health is broken because of my sins.
⁴ My guilt overwhelms me—
  it is a burden too heavy to bear.
⁵ My wounds fester and stink
  because of my foolish sins.
⁶ I am bent over and racked with pain.
  All day long I walk around filled with
  grief.
⁷ A raging fever burns within me,
  and my health is broken.
⁸ I am exhausted and completely crushed.
  My groans come from an anguished
  heart.

⁹ You know what I long for, Lord;
  you hear my every sigh.
¹⁰ My heart beats wildly, my strength fails,
  and I am going blind.
¹¹ My loved ones and friends stay away,
  fearing my disease.
  Even my own family stands at a distance.

¹² Meanwhile, my enemies lay traps to
  kill me.
  Those who wish me harm make plans to
  ruin me.
  All day long they plan their treachery.

¹³ But I am deaf to all their threats.
  I am silent before them as one who
  cannot speak.
¹⁴ I choose to hear nothing,
  and I make no reply.
¹⁵ For I am waiting for you, O LORD.
  You must answer for me, O Lord my
  God.
¹⁶ I prayed, "Don't let my enemies gloat
  over me
  or rejoice at my downfall."

¹⁷ I am on the verge of collapse,
  facing constant pain.
¹⁸ But I confess my sins;
  I am deeply sorry for what I have done.
¹⁹ I have many aggressive enemies;
  they hate me without reason.
²⁰ They repay me evil for good
  and oppose me for pursuing good.
²¹ Do not abandon me, O LORD.
  Do not stand at a distance, my God.
²² Come quickly to help me,
  O Lord my savior.

39

*For Jeduthun, the choir director:
A psalm of David.*

¹ I said to myself, "I will watch what I do
  and not sin in what I say.
  I will hold my tongue
  when the ungodly are around me."
² But as I stood there in silence—
  not even speaking of good things –
  the turmoil within me grew worse.
³ The more I thought about it,
  the hotter I got,
  igniting a fire of words:
⁴ "LORD, remind me how brief my time on
  earth will be.
  Remind me that my days are numbered—
  how fleeting my life is.
⁵ You have made my life no longer than the
  width of my hand.
  My entire lifetime is just a moment to
  you;
  at best, each of us is but a breath."
                                    Interlude

⁶ We are merely moving shadows,
  and all our busy rushing ends in
  nothing.

No Longer Young

OUR DAILY BREAD PSALM 37:23–31

Recently, as I left a shop, I overheard the man who had served me whisper in disappointment, "He called me 'uncle,' when he's definitely older than I am." Since childhood, my Chinese culture has taught me it is polite to say, "Thank you, Uncle!" for help received.

This gesture has served me well, but now I have to think twice before using it. Taking a good look in the mirror, my eyes confirm that I am no longer the person my mind remembers.

Being young has many advantages, but with age comes the joy of reflecting on God's faithfulness. David reminds us in Psalm 37: "Once I was young, and now I am old. Yet I have never seen the godly abandoned" (v. 25).

Now that I'm in my fifties, I reflect and wonder how I ever could have thought that God had forsaken me. Yes, He has permitted me to face what seemed like insurmountable difficulties, but now I know these were only to shape me. God has always preserved me, and when I stumble I know the Lord will keep me from falling. "The Lord directs the steps of the godly. He delights in every detail of their lives. Though they stumble, they will never fall, for the Lord holds them by the hand" (vv. 23–24).

We are growing older all the time, but we can also grow more thankful for God's many mercies. Above all, we are grateful that He puts the love of His law in our hearts and keeps our steps from falling (v. 31). —AL

> The Lord directs the steps of the godly. He delights in every detail of their lives. Though they stumble, they will never fall, for the Lord holds them by the hand.
>
> PSALM 37:23–24

Heavenly Father, your Word tells us that you will keep us from falling. Help us to remember that you care about even the smallest details of life, and you are always there to hold us by your strong hand.

As the years add up, God's faithfulness multiplies.

DAY 8: pg 29

We heap up wealth,
  not knowing who will spend it.
7 And so, Lord, where do I put my hope?
  My only hope is in you.
8 Rescue me from my rebellion.
  Do not let fools mock me.
9 I am silent before you; I won't say a word,
  for my punishment is from you.
10 But please stop striking me!
  I am exhausted by the blows from your hand.

11 When you discipline us for our sins,
  you consume like a moth what is precious to us.
  Each of us is but a breath.   *Interlude*

12 Hear my prayer, O Lord!
  Listen to my cries for help!
  Don't ignore my tears.
  For I am your guest—
  a traveler passing through,
  as my ancestors were before me.
13 Leave me alone so I can smile again
  before I am gone and exist no more.

40
For the choir director:
A psalm of David.

1 I waited patiently for the Lord to help me,
   and he turned to me and heard my cry.
2 He lifted me out of the pit of despair,
   out of the mud and the mire.
   He set my feet on solid ground
   and steadied me as I walked along.
3 He has given me a new song to sing,
   a hymn of praise to our God.
   Many will see what he has done and be
   amazed.
   They will put their trust in the Lord.

4 Oh, the joys of those who trust the Lord,
   who have no confidence in the proud
   or in those who worship idols.
5 O Lord my God, you have performed
   many wonders for us.
   Your plans for us are too numerous to
   list.
   You have no equal.
   If I tried to recite all your wonderful deeds,
   I would never come to the end of them.

6 You take no delight in sacrifices or offerings.
   Now that you have made me listen, I
   finally understand*—
   you don't require burnt offerings or sin
   offerings.
7 Then I said, "Look, I have come.
   As is written about me in the Scriptures:
8 I take joy in doing your will, my God,
   for your instructions are written on my
   heart."

9 I have told all your people about your
   justice.
   I have not been afraid to speak out,
   as you, O Lord, well know.
10 I have not kept the good news of your
   justice hidden in my heart;
   I have talked about your faithfulness
   and saving power.
   I have told everyone in the great assembly
   of your unfailing love and faithfulness.

11 Lord, don't hold back your tender mercies
   from me.
   Let your unfailing love and faithfulness
   always protect me.
12 For troubles surround me—
   too many to count!
   My sins pile up so high
   I can't see my way out.
   They outnumber the hairs on my head.
   I have lost all courage.

13 Please, Lord, rescue me!
   Come quickly, Lord, and help me.
14 May those who try to destroy me
   be humiliated and put to shame.
   May those who take delight in my trouble
   be turned back in disgrace.
15 Let them be horrified by their shame,
   for they said, "Aha! We've got him now!"

16 But may all who search for you
   be filled with joy and gladness in you.
   May those who love your salvation
   repeatedly shout, "The Lord is great!"
17 As for me, since I am poor and needy,
   let the Lord keep me in his thoughts.
   You are my helper and my savior.
   O my God, do not delay.

41
For the choir director: A psalm of David.

1 Oh, the joys of those who are kind to the
   poor!
   The Lord rescues them when they are in
   trouble.
2 The Lord protects them
   and keeps them alive.
   He gives them prosperity in the land
   and rescues them from their enemies.
3 The Lord nurses them when they are sick
   and restores them to health.

4 "O Lord," I prayed, "have mercy on me.
   Heal me, for I have sinned against
   you."
5 But my enemies say nothing but evil
   about me.
   "How soon will he die and be
   forgotten?" they ask.
6 They visit me as if they were my friends,
   but all the while they gather gossip,
   and when they leave, they spread it
   everywhere.
7 All who hate me whisper about me,
   imagining the worst.
8 "He has some fatal disease," they say.
   "He will never get out of that bed!"
9 Even my best friend, the one I trusted
   completely,
   the one who shared my food, has turned
   against me.

10 Lord, have mercy on me.
   Make me well again, so I can pay them
   back!
11 I know you are pleased with me,
   for you have not let my enemies triumph
   over me.

¹² You have preserved my life because I am
   innocent;
      you have brought me into your presence
      forever.

¹³ Praise the LORD, the God of Israel,
      who lives from everlasting to
      everlasting.
   Amen and amen!

BOOK TWO (Psalms 42–72)

42 *For the choir director: A psalm* of the
descendants of Korah.*

¹ As the deer longs for streams of water,
   so I long for you, O God.
² I thirst for God, the living God.
   When can I go and stand before him?
³ Day and night I have only tears for food,
   while my enemies continually taunt me,
      saying,
   "Where is this God of yours?"

⁴ My heart is breaking
   as I remember how it used to be:
I walked among the crowds of
      worshipers,
   leading a great procession to the house
      of God,
singing for joy and giving thanks
   amid the sound of a great celebration!

⁵ Why am I discouraged?
   Why is my heart so sad?
I will put my hope in God!
   I will praise him again—
   my Savior and ⁶my God!

Now I am deeply discouraged,
   but I will remember you—
even from distant Mount Hermon, the
      source of the Jordan,
   from the land of Mount Mizar.
⁷ I hear the tumult of the raging seas
   as your waves and surging tides sweep
      over me.
⁸ But each day the LORD pours his unfailing
      love upon me,
   and through each night I sing his
      songs,
   praying to God who gives me life.

⁹ "O God my rock," I cry,
   "Why have you forgotten me?
Why must I wander around in grief,
   oppressed by my enemies?"
¹⁰ Their taunts break my bones.
   They scoff, "Where is this God of
      yours?"

¹¹ Why am I discouraged?
   Why is my heart so sad?
I will put my hope in God!
   I will praise him again—
   my Savior and my God!

43 ¹ Declare me innocent, O God!
      Defend me against these ungodly
      people.
   Rescue me from these unjust liars.
² For you are God, my only safe haven.
   Why have you tossed me aside?
Why must I wander around in grief,
   oppressed by my enemies?
³ Send out your light and your truth;
   let them guide me.
Let them lead me to your holy mountain,
   to the place where you live.
⁴ There I will go to the altar of God,
   to God—the source of all my joy.
I will praise you with my harp,
   O God, my God!

⁵ Why am I discouraged?
   Why is my heart so sad?
I will put my hope in God!
   I will praise him again—
   my Savior and my God!

44 *For the choir director: A psalm* of the
descendants of Korah.*

¹ O God, we have heard it with our own
      ears—
   our ancestors have told us
of all you did in their day,
   in days long ago:
² You drove out the pagan nations by your
      power
   and gave all the land to our ancestors.
You crushed their enemies
   and set our ancestors free.
³ They did not conquer the land with their
      swords;
   it was not their own strong arm that
      gave them victory.
It was your right hand and strong arm
   and the blinding light from your face
      that helped them,
   for you loved them.

⁴ You are my King and my God.
   You command victories for Israel.*

40:6 Greek text reads *You have given me a body.* Compare Heb 10:5.
42:TITLE Hebrew *maskil.* This may be a literary or musical term.
44:TITLE Hebrew *maskil.* This may be a literary or musical term.
44:4 Hebrew *for Jacob.* The names "Jacob" and "Israel" are often
interchanged throughout the Old Testament, referring sometimes to
the individual patriarch and sometimes to the nation.

⁵ Only by your power can we push back our
  enemies;
    only in your name can we trample our
    foes.
⁶ I do not trust in my bow;
    I do not count on my sword to save me.
⁷ You are the one who gives us victory over
  our enemies;
    you disgrace those who hate us.
⁸ O God, we give glory to you all day long
    and constantly praise your name.

Interlude

⁹ But now you have tossed us aside in
  dishonor.
    You no longer lead our armies to battle.
¹⁰ You make us retreat from our enemies
    and allow those who hate us to plunder
    our land.
¹¹ You have butchered us like sheep
    and scattered us among the nations.
¹² You sold your precious people for a
  pittance,
    making nothing on the sale.
¹³ You let our neighbors mock us.
    We are an object of scorn and derision to
    those around us.
¹⁴ You have made us the butt of their jokes;
    they shake their heads at us in scorn.
¹⁵ We can't escape the constant
  humiliation;
    shame is written across our faces.
¹⁶ All we hear are the taunts of our mockers.
    All we see are our vengeful enemies.

¹⁷ All this has happened though we have not
  forgotten you.
    We have not violated your covenant.
¹⁸ Our hearts have not deserted you.
    We have not strayed from your path.
¹⁹ Yet you have crushed us in the jackal's
  desert home.
    You have covered us with darkness and
    death.
²⁰ If we had forgotten the name of our God
    or spread our hands in prayer to foreign
    gods,
²¹ God would surely have known it,
    for he knows the secrets of every heart.
²² But for your sake we are killed every day;
    we are being slaughtered like sheep.

²³ Wake up, O Lord! Why do you sleep?
    Get up! Do not reject us forever.
²⁴ Why do you look the other way?
    Why do you ignore our suffering and
    oppression?

²⁵ We collapse in the dust,
    lying face down in the dirt.
²⁶ Rise up! Help us!
    Ransom us because of your unfailing
    love.

45 *For the choir director: A love song to be
sung to the tune "Lilies." A psalm**
of the descendants of Korah.

¹ Beautiful words stir my heart.
    I will recite a lovely poem about the
    king,
    for my tongue is like the pen of a skillful
    poet.

² You are the most handsome of all.
    Gracious words stream from your lips.
    God himself has blessed you forever.
³ Put on your sword, O mighty warrior!
    You are so glorious, so majestic!
⁴ In your majesty, ride out to victory,
    defending truth, humility, and justice.
    Go forth to perform awe-inspiring deeds!
⁵ Your arrows are sharp, piercing your
    enemies' hearts.
    The nations fall beneath your feet.

⁶ Your throne, O God,* endures forever and
  ever.
    You rule with a scepter of justice.
⁷ You love justice and hate evil.
    Therefore God, your God, has anointed
    you,
    pouring out the oil of joy on you more
    than on anyone else.
⁸ Myrrh, aloes, and cassia perfume your
  robes.
    In ivory palaces the music of strings
    entertains you.
⁹ Kings' daughters are among your noble
  women.
    At your right side stands the queen,
    wearing jewelry of finest gold from
    Ophir!

¹⁰ Listen to me, O royal daughter; take to
  heart what I say.
    Forget your people and your family far
    away.
¹¹ For your royal husband delights in your
  beauty;
    honor him, for he is your lord.
¹² The princess of Tyre* will shower you with
  gifts.
    The wealthy will beg your favor.
¹³ The bride, a princess, looks glorious
    in her golden gown.

DAY 8

Help!

OUR DAILY BREAD PSALM 46

People are supposed to call 9-1-1 for emergencies only, but many people don't understand or follow the rule. Police emergency operators in Colorado Springs have received calls from people reporting a TV set that wasn't working, asking when it was going to stop snowing, and wanting to report an identification theft while they remained anonymous.

I have often wondered if many of our prayers for help sound frivolous to God. It's impossible to know, but there's one thing we can be assured of: In our times of need, the Lord not only hears our cries, He is present with us.

> **God is our refuge and strength, always ready to help in times of trouble.**
> PSALM 46:1

Psalm 46 describes times of great calamity, including war and natural disasters. Yet it is a song of trust that begins and ends with the same affirmation: "God is our refuge and strength, always ready to help in times of trouble. . . . The LORD of Heaven's Armies is here among us; the God of Israel is our fortress" (vv. 1, 11).

The Lord is always at work accomplishing His purposes—even when the world seems to be falling apart. He tells us, "Be still, and know that I am God! I will be honored by every nation. I will be honored throughout the world" (v. 10).

We don't have to fear. When we call for help, we know that He hears and will come near. —DCM

Help me to know, dear Lord, that no need is too small to bring to your attention. Thank you that you are always there for us, that you are our refuge and strength, and that you are our compassionate Father who comforts us.

God's help is only a prayer away!

DAY 9: pg 33

¹⁴ In her beautiful robes, she is led to the king,
accompanied by her bridesmaids.
¹⁵ What a joyful and enthusiastic procession
as they enter the king's palace!
¹⁶ Your sons will become kings like their father.
You will make them rulers over many lands.
¹⁷ I will bring honor to your name in every generation.
Therefore, the nations will praise you forever and ever.

46 *For the choir director: A song of the descendants of Korah, to be sung by soprano voices.**

¹ God is our refuge and strength,
always ready to help in times of trouble.
² So we will not fear when earthquakes come
and the mountains crumble into the sea.
³ Let the oceans roar and foam.
Let the mountains tremble as the waters surge! *Interlude*

45:TITLE Hebrew *maskil.* This may be a literary or musical term. **45:6** Or *Your divine throne.* **45:12** Hebrew *The daughter of Tyre.* **46:**TITLE Hebrew *according to alamoth.*

⁴ A river brings joy to the city of our God,
the sacred home of the Most High.
⁵ God dwells in that city; it cannot be
destroyed.
From the very break of day, God will
protect it.
⁶ The nations are in chaos,
and their kingdoms crumble!
God's voice thunders,
and the earth melts!
⁷ The LORD of Heaven's Armies is here
among us;
the God of Israel* is our fortress.

Interlude

⁸ Come, see the glorious works of the LORD:
See how he brings destruction upon the
world.
⁹ He causes wars to end throughout the
earth.
He breaks the bow and snaps the
spear;
he burns the shields with fire.
¹⁰ "Be still, and know that I am God!
I will be honored by every nation.
I will be honored throughout the
world."
¹¹ The LORD of Heaven's Armies is here
among us;
the God of Israel is our fortress.

Interlude

47 *For the choir director: A psalm of the
descendants of Korah.*

¹ Come, everyone! Clap your hands!
Shout to God with joyful praise!
² For the LORD Most High is awesome.
He is the great King of all the earth.
³ He subdues the nations before us,
putting our enemies beneath our feet.
⁴ He chose the Promised Land as our
inheritance,
the proud possession of Jacob's
descendants, whom he loves.

Interlude

⁵ God has ascended with a mighty shout.
The LORD has ascended with trumpets
blaring.
⁶ Sing praises to God, sing praises;
sing praises to our King, sing praises!
⁷ For God is the King over all the earth.
Praise him with a psalm.*
⁸ God reigns above the nations,
sitting on his holy throne.

⁹ The rulers of the world have gathered
together
with the people of the God of Abraham.
For all the kings of the earth belong to God.
He is highly honored everywhere.

48 *A song. A psalm of the descendants
of Korah.*

¹ How great is the LORD,
how deserving of praise,
in the city of our God,
which sits on his holy mountain!
² It is high and magnificent;
the whole earth rejoices to see it!
Mount Zion, the holy mountain,*
is the city of the great King!
³ God himself is in Jerusalem's towers,
revealing himself as its defender.

⁴ The kings of the earth joined forces
and advanced against the city.
⁵ But when they saw it, they were stunned;
they were terrified and ran away.
⁶ They were gripped with terror
and writhed in pain like a woman in
labor.
⁷ You destroyed them like the mighty ships
of Tarshish
shattered by a powerful east wind.

⁸ We had heard of the city's glory,
but now we have seen it ourselves—
the city of the LORD of Heaven's Armies.
It is the city of our God;
he will make it safe forever.   *Interlude*

⁹ O God, we meditate on your unfailing love
as we worship in your Temple.
¹⁰ As your name deserves, O God,
you will be praised to the ends of the
earth.
Your strong right hand is filled with
victory.
¹¹ Let the people on Mount Zion rejoice.
Let all the towns of Judah be glad
because of your justice.
¹² Go, inspect the city of Jerusalem.*
Walk around and count the many
towers.
¹³ Take note of the fortified walls,
and tour all the citadels,
that you may describe them
to future generations.
¹⁴ For that is what God is like.
He is our God forever and ever,
and he will guide us until we die.

49

For the choir director: A psalm of the descendants of Korah.

1 Listen to this, all you people!
   Pay attention, everyone in the world!
2 High and low,
   rich and poor—listen!
3 For my words are wise,
   and my thoughts are filled with insight.
4 I listen carefully to many proverbs
   and solve riddles with inspiration from
   a harp.

5 Why should I fear when trouble comes,
   when enemies surround me?
6 They trust in their wealth
   and boast of great riches.
7 Yet they cannot redeem themselves from
   death*
   by paying a ransom to God.
8 Redemption does not come so easily,
   for no one can ever pay enough
9 to live forever
   and never see the grave.

10 Those who are wise must finally die,
   just like the foolish and senseless,
   leaving all their wealth behind.
11 The grave is their eternal home,
   where they will stay forever.
   They may name their estates after
   themselves,
12 but their fame will not last.
   They will die, just like animals.
13 This is the fate of fools,
   though they are remembered as being
   wise.*   *Interlude*

14 Like sheep, they are led to the grave,*
   where death will be their shepherd.
   In the morning the godly will rule over
   them.
   Their bodies will rot in the grave,
   far from their grand estates.
15 But as for me, God will redeem my life.
   He will snatch me from the power of the
   grave.   *Interlude*

16 So don't be dismayed when the wicked
   grow rich
   and their homes become ever more
   splendid.
17 For when they die, they take nothing with
   them.
   Their wealth will not follow them into
   the grave.
18 In this life they consider themselves
   fortunate
   and are applauded for their success.

19 But they will die like all before them
   and never again see the light of day.
20 People who boast of their wealth don't
   understand;
   they will die, just like animals.

50

A psalm of Asaph.

1 The LORD, the Mighty One, is God,
   and he has spoken;
   he has summoned all humanity
   from where the sun rises to where it
   sets.
2 From Mount Zion, the perfection of
   beauty,
   God shines in glorious radiance.
3 Our God approaches,
   and he is not silent.
   Fire devours everything in his way,
   and a great storm rages around him.
4 He calls on the heavens above and earth
   below
   to witness the judgment of his people.
5 "Bring my faithful people to me—
   those who made a covenant with me by
   giving sacrifices."
6 Then let the heavens proclaim his justice,
   for God himself will be the judge.
                                  Interlude

7 "O my people, listen as I speak.
   Here are my charges against you,
   O Israel:
   I am God, your God!
8 I have no complaint about your sacrifices
   or the burnt offerings you constantly
   offer.
9 But I do not need the bulls from your
   barns
   or the goats from your pens.
10 For all the animals of the forest are mine,
   and I own the cattle on a thousand hills.
11 I know every bird on the mountains,
   and all the animals of the field are mine.
12 If I were hungry, I would not tell you,
   for all the world is mine and everything
   in it.
13 Do I eat the meat of bulls?
   Do I drink the blood of goats?
14 Make thankfulness your sacrifice to God,
   and keep the vows you made to the Most
   High.

46:7 Hebrew *of Jacob;* also in 46:11. See note on 44:4.   47:7 Hebrew *maskil.* This may be a literary or musical term.   48:2 Or *Mount Zion, in the far north;* Hebrew reads *Mount Zion, the heights of Zaphon.*
48:12 Hebrew *Zion.*   49:7 Or *no one can redeem the life of another.*
49:13 The meaning of the Hebrew is uncertain.   49:14 Hebrew *Sheol;* also in 49:14b, 15.

¹⁵ Then call on me when you are in trouble,
and I will rescue you,
and you will give me glory."

¹⁶ But God says to the wicked:
"Why bother reciting my decrees
and pretending to obey my covenant?
¹⁷ For you refuse my discipline
and treat my words like trash.
¹⁸ When you see thieves, you approve of
them,
and you spend your time with
adulterers.
¹⁹ Your mouth is filled with wickedness,
and your tongue is full of lies.
²⁰ You sit around and slander your brother—
your own mother's son.
²¹ While you did all this, I remained silent,
and you thought I didn't care.
But now I will rebuke you,
listing all my charges against you.
²² Repent, all of you who forget me,
or I will tear you apart,
and no one will help you.
²³ But giving thanks is a sacrifice that truly
honors me.
If you keep to my path,
I will reveal to you the salvation of
God."

51 *For the choir director: A psalm of David,
regarding the time Nathan the prophet
came to him after David had committed
adultery with Bathsheba.*

¹ Have mercy on me, O God,
because of your unfailing love.
Because of your great compassion,
blot out the stain of my sins.
² Wash me clean from my guilt.
Purify me from my sin.
³ For I recognize my rebellion;
it haunts me day and night.
⁴ Against you, and you alone, have I sinned;
I have done what is evil in your sight.
You will be proved right in what you say,
and your judgment against me is just.*
⁵ For I was born a sinner—
yes, from the moment my mother
conceived me.
⁶ But you desire honesty from the womb,*
teaching me wisdom even there.

⁷ Purify me from my sins,* and I will be
clean;
wash me, and I will be whiter than
snow.

⁸ Oh, give me back my joy again;
you have broken me—
now let me rejoice.
⁹ Don't keep looking at my sins.
Remove the stain of my guilt.
¹⁰ Create in me a clean heart, O God.
Renew a loyal spirit within me.
¹¹ Do not banish me from your presence,
and don't take your Holy Spirit*
from me.

¹² Restore to me the joy of your salvation,
and make me willing to obey you.
¹³ Then I will teach your ways to rebels,
and they will return to you.
¹⁴ Forgive me for shedding blood, O God who
saves;
then I will joyfully sing of your
forgiveness.
¹⁵ Unseal my lips, O Lord,
that my mouth may praise you.

¹⁶ You do not desire a sacrifice, or I would
offer one.
You do not want a burnt offering.
¹⁷ The sacrifice you desire is a broken spirit.
You will not reject a broken and
repentant heart, O God.
¹⁸ Look with favor on Zion and help her;
rebuild the walls of Jerusalem.
¹⁹ Then you will be pleased with sacrifices
offered in the right spirit—
with burnt offerings and whole burnt
offerings.
Then bulls will again be sacrificed on
your altar.

52 *For the choir director: A psalm*
of David, regarding the time Doeg the
Edomite said to Saul, "David has gone to see
Ahimelech."*

¹ Why do you boast about your crimes, great
warrior?
Don't you realize God's justice continues
forever?
² All day long you plot destruction.
Your tongue cuts like a sharp razor;
you're an expert at telling lies.
³ You love evil more than good
and lies more than truth.   *Interlude*

⁴ You love to destroy others with your words,
you liar!
⁵ But God will strike you down once and for
all.
He will pull you from your home
and uproot you from the land of the
living.   *Interlude*

DAY 9

The Old Tractor

OUR DAILY BREAD PSALM 51

My friend Gary restores tractors. He told me about an old John Deere that had been sitting in a farmer's field for years. It had served its owner faithfully for decades.

When Gary was finally able to start the tractor, the engine was in such bad shape that it couldn't have pulled a child's wagon, much less a plow. The belts were cracked, the wires were split, the plugs were rusted, and the carburetor was way out of adjustment.

> **Restore to me the joy of your salvation.**
>
> PSALM 51:12

With loving hands, Gary went to work. He replaced the plugs and points and adjusted the carburetor. When he put it all back together and fired it up, its engine purred like a kitten. It can now pull a plow as strongly as it ever did. Under Gary's restorative skill, it will do all it was designed to do.

In Psalm 51, David repented of his sin with Bathsheba and asked God to restore him to the place of fellowship he once enjoyed. He prayed, "Create in me a clean heart, O God. . . . Restore to me the joy of your salvation" (vv. 10–12).

Through neglect or sin, have you ended up by the wayside spiritually? Turn right now to the Lord. Place yourself in His tender hands. Confess your sin, repent, and ask His forgiveness. He is waiting to restore you to himself and make you a productive Christian again. —DCE

I realize, dear God, that I have let you down—that I have sinned and that I need your forgiveness. Please come alongside me and assure me of your forgiveness and your grace. I need to be restored to the joy of salvation, Lord.

God specializes in restoration.

DAY 10: pg 41

⁶ The righteous will see it and be amazed.
  They will laugh and say,
⁷ "Look what happens to mighty warriors
    who do not trust in God.
  They trust their wealth instead
    and grow more and more bold in their
      wickedness."

⁸ But I am like an olive tree, thriving in the
      house of God.
  I will always trust in God's unfailing
      love.
⁹ I will praise you forever, O God,
    for what you have done.
  I will trust in your good name
    in the presence of your faithful people.

53 *For the choir director: A meditation; a psalm* of David.*

¹ Only fools say in their hearts,
    "There is no God."
  They are corrupt, and their actions are
      evil;
    not one of them does good!

² God looks down from heaven
    on the entire human race;
  he looks to see if anyone is truly wise,
    if anyone seeks God.

51:4 Greek version reads *and you will win your case in court.* Compare Rom 3:4. 51:6 Or *from the heart;* Hebrew reads *in the inward parts.* 51:7 Hebrew *Purify me with the hyssop branch.* 51:11 Or *your spirit of holiness.* 52:TITLE Hebrew *maskil.* This may be a literary or musical term. 53:TITLE Hebrew *According to mahalath; a maskil.* These may be literary or musical terms.

³ But no, all have turned away;
 all have become corrupt.*
No one does good,
 not a single one!

⁴ Will those who do evil never learn?
 They eat up my people like bread
 and wouldn't think of praying to God.
⁵ Terror will grip them,
 terror like they have never known
 before.
God will scatter the bones of your
 enemies.
 You will put them to shame, for God has
 rejected them.

⁶ Who will come from Mount Zion to rescue
 Israel?
 When God restores his people,
 Jacob will shout with joy, and Israel will
 rejoice.

54 *For the choir director: A psalm* of David, regarding the time the Ziphites came and said to Saul, "We know where David is hiding." To be accompanied by stringed instruments.*

¹ Come with great power, O God, and
 rescue me!
 Defend me with your might.
² Listen to my prayer, O God.
 Pay attention to my plea.
³ For strangers are attacking me;
 violent people are trying to kill me.
 They care nothing for God.   *Interlude*

⁴ But God is my helper.
 The Lord keeps me alive!
⁵ May the evil plans of my enemies be
 turned against them.
 Do as you promised and put an end to
 them.

⁶ I will sacrifice a voluntary offering to you;
 I will praise your name, O LORD,
 for it is good.
⁷ For you have rescued me from my troubles
 and helped me to triumph over my
 enemies.

55 *For the choir director: A psalm* of David, to be accompanied by stringed instruments.*

¹ Listen to my prayer, O God.
 Do not ignore my cry for help!
² Please listen and answer me,
 for I am overwhelmed by my troubles.

³ My enemies shout at me,
 making loud and wicked threats.
They bring trouble on me
 and angrily hunt me down.

⁴ My heart pounds in my chest.
 The terror of death assaults me.
⁵ Fear and trembling overwhelm me,
 and I can't stop shaking.
⁶ Oh, that I had wings like a dove;
 then I would fly away and rest!
⁷ I would fly far away
 to the quiet of the wilderness.   *Interlude*
⁸ How quickly I would escape—
 far from this wild storm of hatred.

⁹ Confuse them, Lord, and frustrate their
 plans,
 for I see violence and conflict in the city.
¹⁰ Its walls are patrolled day and night
 against invaders,
 but the real danger is wickedness within
 the city.
¹¹ Everything is falling apart;
 threats and cheating are rampant in the
 streets.

¹² It is not an enemy who taunts me—
 I could bear that.
It is not my foes who so arrogantly
 insult me—
 I could have hidden from them.
¹³ Instead, it is you—my equal,
 my companion and close friend.
¹⁴ What good fellowship we once enjoyed
 as we walked together to the house of
 God.

¹⁵ Let death stalk my enemies;
 let the grave* swallow them alive,
 for evil makes its home within them.

¹⁶ But I will call on God,
 and the LORD will rescue me.
¹⁷ Morning, noon, and night
 I cry out in my distress,
 and the LORD hears my voice.
¹⁸ He ransoms me and keeps me safe
 from the battle waged against me,
 though many still oppose me.
¹⁹ God, who has ruled forever,
 will hear me and humble
 them.   *Interlude*
For my enemies refuse to change their
 ways;
 they do not fear God.

²⁰ As for my companion, he betrayed his
 friends;
 he broke his promises.

21 His words are as smooth as butter,
  but in his heart is war.
His words are as soothing as lotion,
  but underneath are daggers!

22 Give your burdens to the LORD,
  and he will take care of you.
He will not permit the godly to slip and
  fall.

23 But you, O God, will send the wicked
  down to the pit of destruction.
Murderers and liars will die young,
  but I am trusting you to save me.

56

For the choir director: A psalm*
of David, regarding the time the
Philistines seized him in Gath. To be sung to
the tune "Dove on Distant Oaks."

1 O God, have mercy on me,
  for people are hounding me.
My foes attack me all day long.
2 I am constantly hounded by those who
  slander me,
  and many are boldly attacking me.
3 But when I am afraid,
  I will put my trust in you.
4 I praise God for what he has promised.
  I trust in God, so why should I be afraid?
  What can mere mortals do to me?

5 They are always twisting what I say;
  they spend their days plotting to
  harm me.
6 They come together to spy on me—
  watching my every step, eager to kill me.
7 Don't let them get away with their
  wickedness;
  in your anger, O God, bring them down.

8 You keep track of all my sorrows.*
  You have collected all my tears in your
  bottle.
  You have recorded each one in your
  book.

9 My enemies will retreat when I call to you
  for help.
  This I know: God is on my side!
10 I praise God for what he has promised;
  yes, I praise the LORD for what he has
  promised.
11 I trust in God, so why should I be afraid?
  What can mere mortals do to me?

12 I will fulfill my vows to you, O God,
  and will offer a sacrifice of thanks for
  your help.

13 For you have rescued me from death;
  you have kept my feet from slipping.
So now I can walk in your presence,
  O God,
  in your life-giving light.

57

For the choir director: A psalm*
of David, regarding the time he fled
from Saul and went into the cave. To be sung
to the tune "Do Not Destroy!"

1 Have mercy on me, O God, have mercy!
  I look to you for protection.
I will hide beneath the shadow of your
  wings
  until the danger passes by.
2 I cry out to God Most High,*
  to God who will fulfill his purpose
  for me.
3 He will send help from heaven to
  rescue me,
  disgracing those who hound
  me.   *Interlude*
My God will send forth his unfailing love
  and faithfulness.

4 I am surrounded by fierce lions
  who greedily devour human prey—
whose teeth pierce like spears and arrows,
  and whose tongues cut like swords.

5 Be exalted, O God, above the highest
  heavens!
May your glory shine over all the earth.

6 My enemies have set a trap for me.
  I am weary from distress.
They have dug a deep pit in my path,
  but they themselves have fallen into it.
          Interlude

7 My heart is confident in you, O God;
  my heart is confident.
  No wonder I can sing your praises!
8 Wake up, my heart!
  Wake up, O lyre and harp!
  I will wake the dawn with my song.
9 I will thank you, Lord, among all the
  people.
  I will sing your praises among the
  nations.
10 For your unfailing love is as high as the
  heavens.
  Your faithfulness reaches to the clouds.

53:3 Greek version reads *have become useless.* Compare Rom 3:12.
54:TITLE Hebrew *maskil.* This may be a literary or musical term.
55:TITLE Hebrew *maskil.* This may be a literary or musical term.
55:15 Hebrew *let Sheol.* 56:TITLE Hebrew *miktam.* This may be a
literary or musical term. 56:8 Or *my wanderings.* 57:TITLE Hebrew
miktam. This may be a literary or musical term. 57:2 Hebrew
Elohim-Elyon.

11 Be exalted, O God, above the highest
heavens.
May your glory shine over all the earth.

58

For the choir director: A psalm*
of David, to be sung to the tune
"Do Not Destroy!"

1 Justice—do you rulers* know the meaning
of the word?
Do you judge the people fairly?
2 No! You plot injustice in your hearts.
You spread violence throughout the
land.
3 These wicked people are born sinners;
even from birth they have lied and gone
their own way.
4 They spit venom like deadly snakes;
they are like cobras that refuse to listen,
5 ignoring the tunes of the snake charmers,
no matter how skillfully they play.

6 Break off their fangs, O God!
Smash the jaws of these lions,
O LORD!
7 May they disappear like water into thirsty
ground.
Make their weapons useless in their
hands.*
8 May they be like snails that dissolve into
slime,
like a stillborn child who will never see
the sun.
9 God will sweep them away, both young
and old,
faster than a pot heats over burning
thorns.

10 The godly will rejoice when they see
injustice avenged.
They will wash their feet in the blood of
the wicked.
11 Then at last everyone will say,
"There truly is a reward for those who
live for God;
surely there is a God who judges justly
here on earth."

59

For the choir director: A psalm*
of David, regarding the time Saul sent
soldiers to watch David's house in order to kill
him. To be sung to the tune "Do Not Destroy!"

1 Rescue me from my enemies, O God.
Protect me from those who have come to
destroy me.
2 Rescue me from these criminals;
save me from these murderers.

3 They have set an ambush for me.
Fierce enemies are out there waiting,
LORD,
though I have not sinned or offended
them.
4 I have done nothing wrong,
yet they prepare to attack me.
Wake up! See what is happening and
help me!
5 O LORD God of Heaven's Armies, the God
of Israel,
wake up and punish those hostile
nations.
Show no mercy to wicked traitors.
Interlude

6 They come out at night,
snarling like vicious dogs
as they prowl the streets.
7 Listen to the filth that comes from their
mouths;
their words cut like swords.
"After all, who can hear us?" they sneer.
8 But LORD, you laugh at them.
You scoff at all the hostile nations.
9 You are my strength; I wait for you to
rescue me,
for you, O God, are my fortress.
10 In his unfailing love, my God will stand
with me.
He will let me look down in triumph on
all my enemies.

11 Don't kill them, for my people soon forget
such lessons;
stagger them with your power, and
bring them to their knees,
O Lord our shield.
12 Because of the sinful things they say,
because of the evil that is on their lips,
let them be captured by their pride,
their curses, and their lies.
13 Destroy them in your anger!
Wipe them out completely!
Then the whole world will know
that God reigns in Israel.*   *Interlude*

14 My enemies come out at night,
snarling like vicious dogs
as they prowl the streets.
15 They scavenge for food
but go to sleep unsatisfied.*

16 But as for me, I will sing about your power.
Each morning I will sing with joy about
your unfailing love.
For you have been my refuge,
a place of safety when I am in distress.

¹⁷ O my Strength, to you I sing praises,
for you, O God, are my refuge,
the God who shows me unfailing love.

60

For the choir director: A psalm*
of David useful for teaching, regarding
the time David fought Aram-naharaim and
Aram-zobah, and Joab returned and killed
12,000 Edomites in the Valley of Salt. To be
sung to the tune "Lily of the Testimony."

¹ You have rejected us, O God, and broken
our defenses.
You have been angry with us; now
restore us to your favor.
² You have shaken our land and split it
open.
Seal the cracks, for the land trembles.
³ You have been very hard on us,
making us drink wine that sent us
reeling.
⁴ But you have raised a banner for those
who fear you—
a rallying point in the face of attack.
Interlude

⁵ Now rescue your beloved people.
Answer and save us by your power.
⁶ God has promised this by his holiness*:
"I will divide up Shechem with joy.
I will measure out the valley of Succoth.
⁷ Gilead is mine,
and Manasseh, too.
Ephraim, my helmet, will produce my
warriors,
and Judah, my scepter, will produce my
kings.
⁸ But Moab, my washbasin, will become my
servant,
and I will wipe my feet on Edom
and shout in triumph over Philistia."

⁹ Who will bring me into the fortified city?
Who will bring me victory over Edom?
¹⁰ Have you rejected us, O God?
Will you no longer march with our
armies?
¹¹ Oh, please help us against our enemies,
for all human help is useless.
¹² With God's help we will do mighty things,
for he will trample down our foes.

61

For the choir director: A psalm
of David, to be accompanied by
stringed instruments.

¹ O God, listen to my cry!
Hear my prayer!

² From the ends of the earth,
I cry to you for help
when my heart is overwhelmed.
Lead me to the towering rock of safety,
³ for you are my safe refuge,
a fortress where my enemies cannot
reach me.
⁴ Let me live forever in your sanctuary,
safe beneath the shelter of your wings!
Interlude

⁵ For you have heard my vows, O God.
You have given me an inheritance
reserved for those who fear your
name.
⁶ Add many years to the life of the king!
May his years span the generations!
⁷ May he reign under God's protection
forever.
May your unfailing love and faithfulness
watch over him.
⁸ Then I will sing praises to your name
forever
as I fulfill my vows each day.

62

For Jeduthun, the choir director:
A psalm of David.

¹ I wait quietly before God,
for my victory comes from him.
² He alone is my rock and my salvation,
my fortress where I will never be
shaken.

³ So many enemies against one man—
all of them trying to kill me.
To them I'm just a broken-down wall
or a tottering fence.
⁴ They plan to topple me from my high
position.
They delight in telling lies about me.
They praise me to my face
but curse me in their hearts. *Interlude*

⁵ Let all that I am wait quietly before God,
for my hope is in him.
⁶ He alone is my rock and my salvation,
my fortress where I will not be
shaken.
⁷ My victory and honor come from God
alone.
He is my refuge, a rock where no enemy
can reach me.

58:TITLE Hebrew *miktam.* This may be a literary or musical term.
58:1 Or *you gods.* **58:7** Or *Let them be trodden down and wither like*
grass. The meaning of the Hebrew is uncertain. **59:TITLE** Hebrew
miktam. This may be a literary or musical term. **59:13** Hebrew *in*
Jacob. See note on 44:4. **59:15** Or *and growl if they don't get enough.*
60:TITLE Hebrew *miktam.* This may be a literary or musical term.
60:6 Or *in his sanctuary.*

8 O my people, trust in him at all times.
　Pour out your heart to him,
　　for God is our refuge.　　　　*Interlude*

9 Common people are as worthless as a puff
　　of wind,
　and the powerful are not what they
　　appear to be.
　If you weigh them on the scales,
　　together they are lighter than a breath
　　of air.

10 Don't make your living by extortion
　　or put your hope in stealing.
　And if your wealth increases,
　　don't make it the center of your life.

11 God has spoken plainly,
　　and I have heard it many times:
　Power, O God, belongs to you;
12 　unfailing love, O Lord, is yours.
　Surely you repay all people
　　according to what they have done.

63 *A psalm of David, regarding a time
when David was in the wilderness
of Judah.*

1 O God, you are my God;
　I earnestly search for you.
　My soul thirsts for you;
　　my whole body longs for you
　in this parched and weary land
　　where there is no water.
2 I have seen you in your sanctuary
　　and gazed upon your power and glory.
3 Your unfailing love is better than life
　　itself;
　　how I praise you!
4 I will praise you as long as I live,
　　lifting up my hands to you in prayer.
5 You satisfy me more than the richest feast.
　　I will praise you with songs of joy.

6 I lie awake thinking of you,
　　meditating on you through the night.
7 Because you are my helper,
　　I sing for joy in the shadow of your
　　wings.
8 I cling to you;
　　your strong right hand holds me
　　securely.

9 But those plotting to destroy me will come
　　to ruin.
　They will go down into the depths of the
　　earth.
10 They will die by the sword
　　and become the food of jackals.

11 But the king will rejoice in God.
　All who trust in him will praise him,
　　while liars will be silenced.

64 *For the choir director:
A psalm of David.*

1 O God, listen to my complaint.
　Protect my life from my enemies'
　　threats.
2 Hide me from the plots of this evil mob,
　　from this gang of wrongdoers.
3 They sharpen their tongues like swords
　　and aim their bitter words like arrows.
4 They shoot from ambush at the
　　innocent,
　　attacking suddenly and fearlessly.
5 They encourage each other to do evil
　　and plan how to set their traps in
　　secret.
　　"Who will ever notice?" they ask.
6 As they plot their crimes, they say,
　　"We have devised the perfect plan!"
　Yes, the human heart and mind are
　　cunning.

7 But God himself will shoot them with his
　　arrows,
　　suddenly striking them down.
8 Their own tongues will ruin them,
　　and all who see them will shake their
　　heads in scorn.
9 Then everyone will be afraid;
　　they will proclaim the mighty acts of
　　God
　　and realize all the amazing things he
　　does.
10 The godly will rejoice in the LORD
　　and find shelter in him.
　And those who do what is right
　　will praise him.

65 *For the choir director: A song.
A psalm of David.*

1 What mighty praise, O God,
　　belongs to you in Zion.
　We will fulfill our vows to you,
2 　for you answer our prayers.
　All of us must come to you.
3 Though we are overwhelmed by our sins,
　　you forgive them all.
4 What joy for those you choose to bring
　　near,
　　those who live in your holy courts.
　What festivities await us
　　inside your holy Temple.

5 You faithfully answer our prayers with
    awesome deeds,
    O God our savior.
  You are the hope of everyone on earth,
    even those who sail on distant seas.
6 You formed the mountains by your power
    and armed yourself with mighty
    strength.
7 You quieted the raging oceans
    with their pounding waves
    and silenced the shouting of the
    nations.
8 Those who live at the ends of the earth
    stand in awe of your wonders.
  From where the sun rises to where it sets,
    you inspire shouts of joy.

9 You take care of the earth and water it,
    making it rich and fertile.
  The river of God has plenty of water;
    it provides a bountiful harvest of grain,
    for you have ordered it so.
10 You drench the plowed ground with rain,
    melting the clods and leveling the
    ridges.
  You soften the earth with showers
    and bless its abundant crops.
11 You crown the year with a bountiful
    harvest;
    even the hard pathways overflow with
    abundance.
12 The grasslands of the wilderness become
    a lush pasture,
    and the hillsides blossom with joy.
13 The meadows are clothed with flocks of
    sheep,
    and the valleys are carpeted with grain.
    They all shout and sing for joy!

66 For the choir director: A song.
A psalm.

1 Shout joyful praises to God, all the earth!
2   Sing about the glory of his name!
    Tell the world how glorious he is.
3 Say to God, "How awesome are your
    deeds!
    Your enemies cringe before your mighty
    power.
4 Everything on earth will worship you;
    they will sing your praises,
    shouting your name in glorious songs."
                                    Interlude

5 Come and see what our God has done,
    what awesome miracles he performs for
    people!

6 He made a dry path through the Red Sea,*
    and his people went across on foot.
    There we rejoiced in him.
7 For by his great power he rules forever.
    He watches every movement of the
    nations;
    let no rebel rise in defiance.   *Interlude*

8 Let the whole world bless our God
    and loudly sing his praises.
9 Our lives are in his hands,
    and he keeps our feet from stumbling.
10 You have tested us, O God;
    you have purified us like silver.
11 You captured us in your net
    and laid the burden of slavery on our
    backs.
12 Then you put a leader over us.*
    We went through fire and flood,
    but you brought us to a place of great
    abundance.
13 Now I come to your Temple with burnt
    offerings
    to fulfill the vows I made to you—
14 yes, the sacred vows that I made
    when I was in deep trouble.
15 That is why I am sacrificing burnt offerings
    to you—
    the best of my rams as a pleasing aroma,
    and a sacrifice of bulls and male goats.
                                    Interlude

16 Come and listen, all you who fear God,
    and I will tell you what he did for me.
17 For I cried out to him for help,
    praising him as I spoke.
18 If I had not confessed the sin in my heart,
    the Lord would not have listened.
19 But God did listen!
    He paid attention to my prayer.
20 Praise God, who did not ignore my prayer
    or withdraw his unfailing love from me.

67 For the choir director: A song.
A psalm, to be accompanied by
stringed instruments.

1 May God be merciful and bless us.
    May his face smile with favor on us.
                                    Interlude

2 May your ways be known throughout the
    earth,
    your saving power among people
    everywhere.
3 May the nations praise you, O God.
    Yes, may all the nations praise you.

66:6 Hebrew *the sea.* 66:12 Or *You made people ride over our heads.*

⁴ Let the whole world sing for joy,
  because you govern the nations with
    justice
  and guide the people of the whole
    world.   *Interlude*

⁵ May the nations praise you, O God.
  Yes, may all the nations praise you.
⁶ Then the earth will yield its harvests,
  and God, our God, will richly bless us.
⁷ Yes, God will bless us,
  and people all over the world will fear
    him.

68 *For the choir director: A song.
       A psalm of David.*

¹ Rise up, O God, and scatter your enemies.
  Let those who hate God run for their
    lives.
² Blow them away like smoke.
  Melt them like wax in a fire.
  Let the wicked perish in the presence of
    God.
³ But let the godly rejoice.
  Let them be glad in God's presence.
  Let them be filled with joy.
⁴ Sing praises to God and to his name!
  Sing loud praises to him who rides the
    clouds.
  His name is the LORD—
    rejoice in his presence!

⁵ Father to the fatherless, defender of
    widows—
  this is God, whose dwelling is holy.
⁶ God places the lonely in families;
  he sets the prisoners free and gives them
    joy.
  But he makes the rebellious live in a sun-
    scorched land.

⁷ O God, when you led your people out from
    Egypt,
  when you marched through the dry
    wasteland,   *Interlude*
⁸ the earth trembled, and the heavens
    poured down rain
  before you, the God of Sinai,
  before God, the God of Israel.
⁹ You sent abundant rain, O God,
  to refresh the weary land.
¹⁰ There your people finally settled,
  and with a bountiful harvest, O God,
  you provided for your needy people.

¹¹ The Lord gives the word,
  and a great army* brings the good news.

¹² Enemy kings and their armies flee,
  while the women of Israel divide the
    plunder.
¹³ Even those who lived among the
    sheepfolds found treasures—
  doves with wings of silver
  and feathers of gold.
¹⁴ The Almighty scattered the enemy kings
  like a blowing snowstorm on Mount
    Zalmon.

¹⁵ The mountains of Bashan are majestic,
  with many peaks stretching high into
    the sky.
¹⁶ Why do you look with envy, O rugged
    mountains,
  at Mount Zion, where God has chosen
    to live,
  where the LORD himself will live forever?

¹⁷ Surrounded by unnumbered thousands of
    chariots,
  the Lord came from Mount Sinai into his
    sanctuary.
¹⁸ When you ascended to the heights,
  you led a crowd of captives.
  You received gifts from the people,
  even from those who rebelled against
    you.
  Now the LORD God will live among us
    there.

¹⁹ Praise the Lord; praise God our savior!
  For each day he carries us in his
    arms.   *Interlude*
²⁰ Our God is a God who saves!
  The Sovereign LORD rescues us from
    death.

²¹ But God will smash the heads of his
    enemies,
  crushing the skulls of those who love
    their guilty ways.
²² The Lord says, "I will bring my enemies
    down from Bashan;
  I will bring them up from the depths of
    the sea.
²³ You, my people, will wash your feet in
    their blood,
  and even your dogs will get their share!"

²⁴ Your procession has come into view,
    O God—
  the procession of my God and King as he
    goes into the sanctuary.
²⁵ Singers are in front, musicians behind;
  between them are young women playing
    tambourines.

Keep On

OUR DAILY BREAD PSALM 66

"Keep on travelin'. Keep on . . ." sang the teenagers of the chorale. They had just sung the first five words of their Sunday evening concert when everything went dark. All power was gone.

Well, not all power. Not true power.

The students kept singing. Some people went and found flashlights to shine on the chorale as they sang their entire repertoire without their taped accompaniment.

Midway through the concert, the director asked the congregation to sing along. It was goose bumps time as God's name was lifted high in that darkened church. "Hallelujah" never seemed so heavenly.

Before the concert, everyone had worked hard to make sure all the electrical equipment was working. But the best thing that happened was for that power to go out. As a result, God's power was highlighted. God's light, not electric light, shone through. Jesus was praised.

Sometimes our plans break down and our efforts fall short. When things happen that we can't control, we must "keep on travelin'" and remember where the real power for godly living and true praise comes from. When our efforts falter, we need to keep praising and lifting up Jesus. It's all about Him anyway. —JDB

> Everything on earth will worship you; they will sing your praises, shouting your name in glorious songs.
>
> PSALM 66:4

We shout our joyful praises to you, O God! When we encounter obstacles, it is you alone on whom we can depend. You are all-powerful, and there is none greater than you.

God's great power deserves our grateful praise.

DAY 11: pg 45

26 Praise God, all you people of Israel; praise the LORD, the source of Israel's life.
27 Look, the little tribe of Benjamin leads the way.
Then comes a great throng of rulers from Judah
and all the rulers of Zebulun and Naphtali.
28 Summon your might, O God.
Display your power, O God, as you have in the past.
29 The kings of the earth are bringing tribute
to your Temple in Jerusalem.

30 Rebuke these enemy nations—
these wild animals lurking in the reeds,
this herd of bulls among the weaker calves.
Make them bring bars of silver in humble tribute.
Scatter the nations that delight in war.
31 Let Egypt come with gifts of precious metals*;
let Ethiopia* bow in submission to God.
32 Sing to God, you kingdoms of the earth.
Sing praises to the Lord. *Interlude*

68:11 Or *a host of women.* 68:31a Or *of rich cloth.* 68:31b Hebrew *Cush.*

³³ Sing to the one who rides across the
ancient heavens,
his mighty voice thundering from the sky.
³⁴ Tell everyone about God's power.
His majesty shines down on Israel;
his strength is mighty in the heavens.
³⁵ God is awesome in his sanctuary.
The God of Israel gives power and
strength to his people.

Praise be to God!

69

*For the choir director: A psalm
of David, to be sung to the tune "Lilies."*

¹ Save me, O God,
for the floodwaters are up to my neck.
² Deeper and deeper I sink into the mire;
I can't find a foothold.
I am in deep water,
and the floods overwhelm me.
³ I am exhausted from crying for help;
my throat is parched.
My eyes are swollen with weeping,
waiting for my God to help me.
⁴ Those who hate me without cause
outnumber the hairs on my head.
Many enemies try to destroy me with lies,
demanding that I give back what I didn't
steal.

⁵ O God, you know how foolish I am;
my sins cannot be hidden from you.
⁶ Don't let those who trust in you be
ashamed because of me,
O Sovereign LORD of Heaven's Armies.
Don't let me cause them to be humiliated,
O God of Israel.
⁷ For I endure insults for your sake;
humiliation is written all over my face.
⁸ Even my own brothers pretend they don't
know me;
they treat me like a stranger.

⁹ Passion for your house has consumed me,
and the insults of those who insult you
have fallen on me.
¹⁰ When I weep and fast,
they scoff at me.
¹¹ When I dress in burlap to show sorrow,
they make fun of me.
¹² I am the favorite topic of town gossip,
and all the drunks sing about me.

¹³ But I keep praying to you, LORD,
hoping this time you will show me favor.
In your unfailing love, O God,
answer my prayer with your sure
salvation.

¹⁴ Rescue me from the mud;
don't let me sink any deeper!
Save me from those who hate me,
and pull me from these deep waters.
¹⁵ Don't let the floods overwhelm me,
or the deep waters swallow me,
or the pit of death devour me.

¹⁶ Answer my prayers, O LORD,
for your unfailing love is wonderful.
Take care of me,
for your mercy is so plentiful.
¹⁷ Don't hide from your servant;
answer me quickly, for I am in deep
trouble!
¹⁸ Come and redeem me;
free me from my enemies.

¹⁹ You know of my shame, scorn, and
disgrace.
You see all that my enemies are doing.
²⁰ Their insults have broken my heart,
and I am in despair.
If only one person would show some pity;
if only one would turn and comfort me.
²¹ But instead, they give me poison* for food;
they offer me sour wine for my thirst.

²² Let the bountiful table set before them
become a snare
and their prosperity become a trap.*
²³ Let their eyes go blind so they cannot see,
and make their bodies shake
continually.*
²⁴ Pour out your fury on them;
consume them with your burning anger.
²⁵ Let their homes become desolate
and their tents be deserted.
²⁶ To the one you have punished, they add
insult to injury;
they add to the pain of those you have
hurt.
²⁷ Pile their sins up high,
and don't let them go free.
²⁸ Erase their names from the Book of Life;
don't let them be counted among the
righteous.

²⁹ I am suffering and in pain.
Rescue me, O God, by your saving power.

³⁰ Then I will praise God's name with
singing,
and I will honor him with thanksgiving.
³¹ For this will please the LORD more than
sacrificing cattle,
more than presenting a bull with its
horns and hooves.

³² The humble will see their God at work and
be glad.
Let all who seek God's help be
encouraged.
³³ For the LORD hears the cries of the needy;
he does not despise his imprisoned
people.

³⁴ Praise him, O heaven and earth,
the seas and all that move in them.
³⁵ For God will save Jerusalem*
and rebuild the towns of Judah.
His people will live there
and settle in their own land.
³⁶ The descendants of those who obey him
will inherit the land,
and those who love him will live there
in safety.

70

*For the choir director: A psalm
of David, asking God to remember him.*

¹ Please, God, rescue me!
Come quickly, LORD, and help me.
² May those who try to kill me
be humiliated and put to shame.
May those who take delight in my trouble
be turned back in disgrace.
³ Let them be horrified by their shame,
for they said, "Aha! We've got him
now!"
⁴ But may all who search for you
be filled with joy and gladness in you.
May those who love your salvation
repeatedly shout, "God is great!"
⁵ But as for me, I am poor and needy;
please hurry to my aid, O God.
You are my helper and my savior;
O LORD, do not delay.

71

¹ O LORD, I have come to you for
protection;
don't let me be disgraced.
² Save me and rescue me,
for you do what is right.
Turn your ear to listen to me,
and set me free.
³ Be my rock of safety
where I can always hide.
Give the order to save me,
for you are my rock and my fortress.
⁴ My God, rescue me from the power of the
wicked,
from the clutches of cruel oppressors.
⁵ O Lord, you alone are my hope.
I've trusted you, O LORD, from
childhood.

⁶ Yes, you have been with me from birth;
from my mother's womb you have cared
for me.
No wonder I am always praising you!
⁷ My life is an example to many,
because you have been my strength and
protection.
⁸ That is why I can never stop praising you;
I declare your glory all day long.
⁹ And now, in my old age, don't set me
aside.
Don't abandon me when my strength is
failing.
¹⁰ For my enemies are whispering
against me.
They are plotting together to kill me.
¹¹ They say, "God has abandoned him.
Let's go and get him,
for no one will help him now."

¹² O God, don't stay away.
My God, please hurry to help me.
¹³ Bring disgrace and destruction on my
accusers.
Humiliate and shame those who want to
harm me.
¹⁴ But I will keep on hoping for your help;
I will praise you more and more.
¹⁵ I will tell everyone about your
righteousness.
All day long I will proclaim your saving
power,
though I am not skilled with words.*
¹⁶ I will praise your mighty deeds,
O Sovereign LORD.
I will tell everyone that you alone are
just.

¹⁷ O God, you have taught me from my
earliest childhood,
and I constantly tell others about the
wonderful things you do.
¹⁸ Now that I am old and gray,
do not abandon me, O God.
Let me proclaim your power to this new
generation,
your mighty miracles to all who come
after me.

¹⁹ Your righteousness, O God, reaches to the
highest heavens.
You have done such wonderful things.
Who can compare with you, O God?

69:21 Or *gall.* **69:22** Greek version reads *Let their bountiful table set
before them become a snare, / a trap that makes them think all is well.
/ Let their blessings cause them to stumble, / and let them get what
they deserve.* Compare Rom 11:9. **69:23** Greek version reads *and let
their backs be bent forever.* Compare Rom 11:10. **69:35** Hebrew *Zion.*
71:15 Or *though I cannot count it.*

²⁰ You have allowed me to suffer much
hardship,
but you will restore me to life again
and lift me up from the depths of the
earth.
²¹ You will restore me to even greater honor
and comfort me once again.

²² Then I will praise you with music on the
harp,
because you are faithful to your
promises, O my God.
I will sing praises to you with a lyre,
O Holy One of Israel.
²³ I will shout for joy and sing your praises,
for you have ransomed me.
²⁴ I will tell about your righteous deeds
all day long,
for everyone who tried to hurt me
has been shamed and humiliated.

72 A psalm of Solomon.

¹ Give your love of justice to the king, O God,
and righteousness to the king's son.
² Help him judge your people in the right
way;
let the poor always be treated fairly.
³ May the mountains yield prosperity
for all,
and may the hills be fruitful.
⁴ Help him to defend the poor,
to rescue the children of the needy,
and to crush their oppressors.
⁵ May they fear you* as long as the sun
shines,
as long as the moon remains in the sky.
Yes, forever!

⁶ May the king's rule be refreshing like
spring rain on freshly cut grass,
like the showers that water the earth.
⁷ May all the godly flourish during his reign.
May there be abundant prosperity until
the moon is no more.
⁸ May he reign from sea to sea,
and from the Euphrates River* to the
ends of the earth.
⁹ Desert nomads will bow before him;
his enemies will fall before him in the
dust.
¹⁰ The western kings of Tarshish and other
distant lands
will bring him tribute.
The eastern kings of Sheba and Seba
will bring him gifts.

¹¹ All kings will bow before him,
and all nations will serve him.
¹² He will rescue the poor when they cry to
him;
he will help the oppressed, who have no
one to defend them.
¹³ He feels pity for the weak and the needy,
and he will rescue them.
¹⁴ He will redeem them from oppression and
violence,
for their lives are precious to him.

¹⁵ Long live the king!
May the gold of Sheba be given to him.
May the people always pray for him
and bless him all day long.
¹⁶ May there be abundant grain throughout
the land,
flourishing even on the hilltops.
May the fruit trees flourish like the trees of
Lebanon,
and may the people thrive like grass in
a field.
¹⁷ May the king's name endure forever;
may it continue as long as the sun shines.
May all nations be blessed through him
and bring him praise.

¹⁸ Praise the LORD God, the God of Israel,
who alone does such wonderful things.
¹⁹ Praise his glorious name forever!
Let the whole earth be filled with his
glory.
Amen and amen!

²⁰ (This ends the prayers of David son of
Jesse.)

BOOK THREE (Psalms 73–89)

73 A psalm of Asaph.

¹ Truly God is good to Israel,
to those whose hearts are pure.
² But as for me, I almost lost my footing.
My feet were slipping, and I was almost
gone.
³ For I envied the proud
when I saw them prosper despite their
wickedness.
⁴ They seem to live such painless lives;
their bodies are so healthy and strong.
⁵ They don't have troubles like other people;
they're not plagued with problems like
everyone else.
⁶ They wear pride like a jeweled necklace
and clothe themselves with cruelty.
⁷ These fat cats have everything
their hearts could ever wish for!

When Life Seems Unfair

OUR DAILY BREAD PSALM 73

Have you ever felt that life is unfair? For those of us who are committed to following the will and ways of Jesus, it's easy to get frustrated when people who don't care about Him seem to do well in life. A businessman cheats yet wins a large contract, and the guy who parties all the time is robust and healthy—while you or your loved ones struggle with finances or medical issues. It makes us feel cheated, like maybe we've been good for nothing.

If you've ever felt that way, you're in good company. The writer of Psalm 73 goes through a whole list of how the wicked prosper, and then he asks, "Did I keep my heart pure for nothing? Did I keep myself innocent for no reason?" (v. 13). But the tide of his thoughts turns when he recalls his time in God's presence: "I finally understood the destiny of the wicked" (v. 17).

> I envied the proud when I saw them prosper despite their wickedness.
>
> PSALM 73:3

When we spend time with God and see things from His point of view, it changes our perspective completely. We may be jealous of the nonbelievers now, but we won't be at judgment time. As the saying goes, what difference does it make if you win the battle but lose the war?

Like the psalmist, let's praise God for His presence in this life and His promise of the life to come (vv. 25–28). He is all you need, even when life seems unfair. —JMS

Dear God, even when life seems unfair, I have the assurance that with you as my Lord, I am promised eternal life. There's absolutely nothing better than that.

Spending time with God puts everything else in perspective.

DAY 12: pg 49

8 They scoff and speak only evil;
   in their pride they seek to crush others.
9 They boast against the very heavens,
   and their words strut throughout the earth.
10 And so the people are dismayed and confused,
   drinking in all their words.
11 "What does God know?" they ask.
   "Does the Most High even know what's happening?"
12 Look at these wicked people—
   enjoying a life of ease while their riches multiply.

13 Did I keep my heart pure for nothing?
   Did I keep myself innocent for no reason?
14 I get nothing but trouble all day long;
   every morning brings me pain.
15 If I had really spoken this way to others,
   I would have been a traitor to your people.
16 So I tried to understand why the wicked prosper.
   But what a difficult task it is!
17 Then I went into your sanctuary, O God,
   and I finally understood the destiny of the wicked.

72:5 Greek version reads *May they endure.* 72:8 Hebrew *the river.*

18 Truly, you put them on a slippery path
and send them sliding over the cliff to
destruction.
19 In an instant they are destroyed,
completely swept away by terrors.
20 When you arise, O Lord,
you will laugh at their silly ideas
as a person laughs at dreams in the
morning.

21 Then I realized that my heart was bitter,
and I was all torn up inside.
22 I was so foolish and ignorant—
I must have seemed like a senseless
animal to you.
23 Yet I still belong to you;
you hold my right hand.
24 You guide me with your counsel,
leading me to a glorious destiny.
25 Whom have I in heaven but you?
I desire you more than anything on
earth.
26 My health may fail, and my spirit may
grow weak,
but God remains the strength of my
heart;
he is mine forever.

27 Those who desert him will perish,
for you destroy those who abandon you.
28 But as for me, how good it is to be near
God!
I have made the Sovereign LORD my
shelter,
and I will tell everyone about the
wonderful things you do.

74 A psalm* of Asaph.

1 O God, why have you rejected us so long?
Why is your anger so intense against the
sheep of your own pasture?
2 Remember that we are the people you
chose long ago,
the tribe you redeemed as your own
special possession!
And remember Jerusalem,* your home
here on earth.
3 Walk through the awful ruins of the city;
see how the enemy has destroyed your
sanctuary.

4 There your enemies shouted their
victorious battle cries;
there they set up their battle standards.
5 They swung their axes
like woodcutters in a forest.

6 With axes and picks,
they smashed the carved paneling.
7 They burned your sanctuary to the
ground.
They defiled the place that bears your
name.
8 Then they thought, "Let's destroy
everything!"
So they burned down all the places
where God was worshiped.

9 We no longer see your miraculous signs.
All the prophets are gone,
and no one can tell us when it will end.
10 How long, O God, will you allow our
enemies to insult you?
Will you let them dishonor your name
forever?
11 Why do you hold back your strong right
hand?
Unleash your powerful fist and destroy
them.

12 You, O God, are my king from ages past,
bringing salvation to the earth.
13 You split the sea by your strength
and smashed the heads of the sea
monsters.
14 You crushed the heads of Leviathan*
and let the desert animals eat him.
15 You caused the springs and streams to
gush forth,
and you dried up rivers that never run
dry.
16 Both day and night belong to you;
you made the starlight* and the sun.
17 You set the boundaries of the earth,
and you made both summer and winter.

18 See how these enemies insult you, LORD.
A foolish nation has dishonored your
name.
19 Don't let these wild beasts destroy your
turtledoves.
Don't forget your suffering people
forever.

20 Remember your covenant promises,
for the land is full of darkness and
violence!
21 Don't let the downtrodden be humiliated
again.
Instead, let the poor and needy praise
your name.

22 Arise, O God, and defend your cause.
Remember how these fools insult you
all day long.

²³ Don't overlook what your enemies have
said
or their growing uproar.

75 *For the choir director: A psalm
of Asaph. A song to be sung to the tune
"Do Not Destroy!"*

¹ We thank you, O God!
We give thanks because you are near.
People everywhere tell of your
wonderful deeds.

² God says, "At the time I have planned,
I will bring justice against the wicked.
³ When the earth quakes and its people live
in turmoil,
I am the one who keeps its foundations
firm. *Interlude*

⁴ "I warned the proud, 'Stop your boasting!'
I told the wicked, 'Don't raise your fists!
⁵ Don't raise your fists in defiance at the
heavens
or speak with such arrogance.'"
⁶ For no one on earth—from east or west,
or even from the wilderness—
should raise a defiant fist.*
⁷ It is God alone who judges;
he decides who will rise and who will
fall.
⁸ For the LORD holds a cup in his hand
that is full of foaming wine mixed with
spices.
He pours out the wine in judgment,
and all the wicked must drink it,
draining it to the dregs.

⁹ But as for me, I will always proclaim what
God has done;
I will sing praises to the God of Jacob.
¹⁰ For God says, "I will break the strength of
the wicked,
but I will increase the power of the
godly."

76 *For the choir director: A psalm
of Asaph. A song to be accompanied
by stringed instruments.*

¹ God is honored in Judah;
his name is great in Israel.
² Jerusalem* is where he lives;
Mount Zion is his home.
³ There he has broken the fiery arrows of the
enemy,
the shields and swords and weapons of
war. *Interlude*

⁴ You are glorious and more majestic
than the everlasting mountains.*
⁵ Our boldest enemies have been plundered.
They lie before us in the sleep of death.
No warrior could lift a hand against us.
⁶ At the blast of your breath, O God of Jacob,
their horses and chariots lay still.

⁷ No wonder you are greatly feared!
Who can stand before you when your
anger explodes?
⁸ From heaven you sentenced your enemies;
the earth trembled and stood silent
before you.
⁹ You stand up to judge those who do evil,
O God,
and to rescue the oppressed of the
earth. *Interlude*
¹⁰ Human defiance only enhances your
glory,
for you use it as a weapon.*

¹¹ Make vows to the LORD your God, and
keep them.
Let everyone bring tribute to the
Awesome One.
¹² For he breaks the pride of princes,
and the kings of the earth fear him.

77 *For Jeduthun, the choir director:
A psalm of Asaph.*

¹ I cry out to God; yes, I shout.
Oh, that God would listen to me!
² When I was in deep trouble,
I searched for the Lord.
All night long I prayed, with hands lifted
toward heaven,
but my soul was not comforted.
³ I think of God, and I moan,
overwhelmed with longing for his help.
Interlude

⁴ You don't let me sleep.
I am too distressed even to pray!
⁵ I think of the good old days,
long since ended,
⁶ when my nights were filled with joyful
songs.
I search my soul and ponder the
difference now.
⁷ Has the Lord rejected me forever?
Will he never again be kind to me?

74:TITLE Hebrew *maskil.* This may be a literary or musical term.
74:2 Hebrew *Mount Zion.* 74:14 The identification of Leviathan is
disputed, ranging from an earthly creature to a mythical sea monster
in ancient literature. 74:16 Or *moon;* Hebrew reads *light.* 75:6 Hebrew
should lift. 76:2 Hebrew *Salem,* another name for Jerusalem. 76:4 As
in Greek version; Hebrew reads *than mountains filled with beasts of
prey.* 76:10 The meaning of the Hebrew is uncertain.

8 Is his unfailing love gone forever?
  Have his promises permanently
  failed?
9 Has God forgotten to be gracious?
  Has he slammed the door on his
  compassion?   *Interlude*

10 And I said, "This is my fate;
  the Most High has turned his hand
  against me."
11 But then I recall all you have done,
  O LORD;
  I remember your wonderful deeds of
  long ago.
12 They are constantly in my thoughts.
  I cannot stop thinking about your
  mighty works.

13 O God, your ways are holy.
  Is there any god as mighty as you?
14 You are the God of great wonders!
  You demonstrate your awesome power
  among the nations.
15 By your strong arm, you redeemed your
  people,
  the descendants of Jacob and Joseph.
                                Interlude

16 When the Red Sea* saw you, O God,
  its waters looked and trembled!
  The sea quaked to its very depths.
17 The clouds poured down rain;
  the thunder rumbled in the sky.
  Your arrows of lightning flashed.
18 Your thunder roared from the
  whirlwind;
  the lightning lit up the world!
  The earth trembled and shook.
19 Your road led through the sea,
  your pathway through the mighty
  waters—
  a pathway no one knew was there!
20 You led your people along that road like a
  flock of sheep,
  with Moses and Aaron as their
  shepherds.

78 *A psalm* of Asaph.*

1 O my people, listen to my instructions.
  Open your ears to what I am saying,
2   for I will speak to you in a parable.
  I will teach you hidden lessons from our
  past—
3   stories we have heard and known,
  stories our ancestors handed down
  to us.

4 We will not hide these truths from our
  children;
  we will tell the next generation
  about the glorious deeds of the LORD,
  about his power and his mighty
  wonders.
5 For he issued his laws to Jacob;
  he gave his instructions to Israel.
  He commanded our ancestors
  to teach them to their children,
6 so the next generation might know them—
  even the children not yet born—
  and they in turn will teach their own
  children.
7 So each generation should set its hope
  anew on God,
  not forgetting his glorious miracles
  and obeying his commands.
8 Then they will not be like their ancestors—
  stubborn, rebellious, and unfaithful,
  refusing to give their hearts to God.

9 The warriors of Ephraim, though armed
  with bows,
  turned their backs and fled on the day
  of battle.
10 They did not keep God's covenant
  and refused to live by his instructions.
11 They forgot what he had done—
  the great wonders he had shown them,
12 the miracles he did for their ancestors
  on the plain of Zoan in the land of
  Egypt.
13 For he divided the sea and led them
  through,
  making the water stand up like walls!
14 In the daytime he led them by a cloud,
  and all night by a pillar of fire.
15 He split open the rocks in the wilderness
  to give them water, as from a gushing
  spring.
16 He made streams pour from the rock,
  making the waters flow down like a river!

17 Yet they kept on sinning against him,
  rebelling against the Most High in the
  desert.
18 They stubbornly tested God in their hearts,
  demanding the foods they craved.
19 They even spoke against God himself,
  saying,
  "God can't give us food in the
  wilderness.
20 Yes, he can strike a rock so water gushes
  out,
  but he can't give his people bread and
  meat."

A Child's Wonder

OUR DAILY BREAD PSALM 78:1–8

In nineteenth-century Scotland, a young mother observed her three-year-old son's inquisitive nature. It seemed he was curious about everything that moved or made a noise. James Clerk Maxwell would carry his boyhood wonder with him into a remarkable career in science. He went on to do groundbreaking work in electricity and magnetism. Years later, Albert Einstein would say of Maxwell's work that it was "the most fruitful that physics has experienced since the time of Newton."

From early childhood, religion touched all aspects of Maxwell's life. As a committed Christian, he prayed: "Teach us to study the works of Thy hands . . . and strengthen our reason for Thy service." The boyhood cultivation of Maxwell's spiritual life and curiosity resulted in a lifetime of using science in service to the Creator.

The community of faith has always had the responsibility to nurture the talent of the younger generation and to orient their lives to the Lord, "so each generation should set its hope anew on God, not forgetting his glorious miracles and obeying his commands" (Ps 78:7).

Finding ways to encourage children's love for learning while establishing them in the faith is an important investment in the future. —HDF

> [God] issued his laws to Jacob; he gave his instructions to Israel. He commanded our ancestors to teach them to their children, so the next generation might know them—even the children not yet born—and they in turn will teach their own children.
>
> PSALM 78:5–6

Fill us, Lord Jesus, with a sense of childlike wonder. Thank you for giving us the privilege to teach a younger generation the magnificence of your creation. Give us the desire and ability to teach these little ones to grow in the knowledge of your world and in their love for you. Amen.

We shape tomorrow's world by what we teach our children today.

DAY 13: pg 55

21 When the LORD heard them, he was
    furious.
  The fire of his wrath burned against
    Jacob.
  Yes, his anger rose against Israel,
22 for they did not believe God
    or trust him to care for them.
23 But he commanded the skies to open;
  he opened the doors of heaven.
24 He rained down manna for them to eat;
  he gave them bread from heaven.

25 They ate the food of angels!
    God gave them all they could hold.
26 He released the east wind in the
    heavens
  and guided the south wind by his
    mighty power.
27 He rained down meat as thick as
    dust—
  birds as plentiful as the sand on the
    seashore!

77:16 Hebrew *the waters.* 78:TITLE Hebrew *maskil.* This may be a literary or musical term.

28 He caused the birds to fall within their
camp
and all around their tents.
29 The people ate their fill.
He gave them what they craved.
30 But before they satisfied their craving,
while the meat was yet in their mouths,
31 the anger of God rose against them,
and he killed their strongest men.
He struck down the finest of Israel's
young men.

32 But in spite of this, the people kept
sinning.
Despite his wonders, they refused to
trust him.
33 So he ended their lives in failure,
their years in terror.
34 When God began killing them,
they finally sought him.
They repented and took God seriously.
35 Then they remembered that God was their
rock,
that God Most High* was their redeemer.
36 But all they gave him was lip service;
they lied to him with their tongues.
37 Their hearts were not loyal to him.
They did not keep his covenant.
38 Yet he was merciful and forgave their sins
and did not destroy them all.
Many times he held back his anger
and did not unleash his fury!
39 For he remembered that they were merely
mortal,
gone like a breath of wind that never
returns.

40 Oh, how often they rebelled against him in
the wilderness
and grieved his heart in that dry
wasteland.
41 Again and again they tested God's
patience
and provoked the Holy One of Israel.
42 They did not remember his power
and how he rescued them from their
enemies.
43 They did not remember his miraculous
signs in Egypt,
his wonders on the plain of Zoan.
44 For he turned their rivers into blood,
so no one could drink from the streams.
45 He sent vast swarms of flies to consume
them
and hordes of frogs to ruin them.
46 He gave their crops to caterpillars;
their harvest was consumed by locusts.

47 He destroyed their grapevines with hail
and shattered their sycamore-figs with
sleet.
48 He abandoned their cattle to the hail,
their livestock to bolts of lightning.
49 He loosed on them his fierce anger—
all his fury, rage, and hostility.
He dispatched against them
a band of destroying angels.
50 He turned his anger against them;
he did not spare the Egyptians' lives
but ravaged them with the plague.
51 He killed the oldest son in each Egyptian
family,
the flower of youth throughout the land
of Egypt.*
52 But he led his own people like a flock of
sheep,
guiding them safely through the
wilderness.
53 He kept them safe so they were not
afraid;
but the sea covered their enemies.
54 He brought them to the border of his holy
land,
to this land of hills he had won for
them.
55 He drove out the nations before them;
he gave them their inheritance by lot.
He settled the tribes of Israel into their
homes.

56 But they kept testing and rebelling against
God Most High.
They did not obey his laws.
57 They turned back and were as faithless as
their parents.
They were as undependable as a
crooked bow.
58 They angered God by building shrines to
other gods;
they made him jealous with their idols.
59 When God heard them, he was very angry,
and he completely rejected Israel.
60 Then he abandoned his dwelling at
Shiloh,
the Tabernacle where he had lived
among the people.
61 He allowed the Ark of his might to be
captured;
he surrendered his glory into enemy
hands.
62 He gave his people over to be butchered by
the sword,
because he was so angry with his own
people—his special possession.

⁶³ Their young men were killed by fire;
their young women died before singing
their wedding songs.
⁶⁴ Their priests were slaughtered,
and their widows could not mourn their
deaths.

⁶⁵ Then the Lord rose up as though waking
from sleep,
like a warrior aroused from a drunken
stupor.
⁶⁶ He routed his enemies
and sent them to eternal shame.
⁶⁷ But he rejected Joseph's descendants;
he did not choose the tribe of Ephraim.
⁶⁸ He chose instead the tribe of Judah,
and Mount Zion, which he loved.
⁶⁹ There he built his sanctuary as high as the
heavens,
as solid and enduring as the earth.
⁷⁰ He chose his servant David,
calling him from the sheep pens.
⁷¹ He took David from tending the ewes and
lambs
and made him the shepherd of Jacob's
descendants—
God's own people, Israel.
⁷² He cared for them with a true heart
and led them with skillful hands.

79 A psalm of Asaph.

¹ O God, pagan nations have conquered
your land,
your special possession.
They have defiled your holy Temple
and made Jerusalem a heap of ruins.
² They have left the bodies of your servants
as food for the birds of heaven.
The flesh of your godly ones
has become food for the wild animals.
³ Blood has flowed like water all around
Jerusalem;
no one is left to bury the dead.
⁴ We are mocked by our neighbors,
an object of scorn and derision to those
around us.

⁵ O LORD, how long will you be angry with
us? Forever?
How long will your jealousy burn like
fire?
⁶ Pour out your wrath on the nations that
refuse to acknowledge you—
on kingdoms that do not call upon your
name.

⁷ For they have devoured your people
Israel,*
making the land a desolate wilderness.
⁸ Do not hold us guilty for the sins of our
ancestors!
Let your compassion quickly meet our
needs,
for we are on the brink of despair.

⁹ Help us, O God of our salvation!
Help us for the glory of your name.
Save us and forgive our sins
for the honor of your name.
¹⁰ Why should pagan nations be allowed to
scoff,
asking, "Where is their God?"
Show us your vengeance against the
nations,
for they have spilled the blood of your
servants.
¹¹ Listen to the moaning of the prisoners.
Demonstrate your great power by saving
those condemned to die.

¹² O Lord, pay back our neighbors seven times
for the scorn they have hurled at you.
¹³ Then we your people, the sheep of your
pasture,
will thank you forever and ever,
praising your greatness from generation
to generation.

80 For the choir director: A psalm of Asaph, to be sung to the tune "Lilies of the Covenant."

¹ Please listen, O Shepherd of Israel,
you who lead Joseph's descendants like
a flock.
O God, enthroned above the cherubim,
display your radiant glory
² to Ephraim, Benjamin, and Manasseh.
Show us your mighty power.
Come to rescue us!

³ Turn us again to yourself, O God.
Make your face shine down upon us.
Only then will we be saved.
⁴ O LORD God of Heaven's Armies,
how long will you be angry with our
prayers?
⁵ You have fed us with sorrow
and made us drink tears by the
bucketful.
⁶ You have made us the scorn* of
neighboring nations.
Our enemies treat us as a joke.

78:35 Hebrew El-Elyon. 78:51 Hebrew in the tents of Ham.
79:7 Hebrew devoured Jacob. See note on 44:4. 80:6 As in Syriac
version; Hebrew reads the strife.

⁷ Turn us again to yourself, O God of
Heaven's Armies.
Make your face shine down upon us.
Only then will we be saved.
⁸ You brought us from Egypt like a
grapevine;
you drove away the pagan nations and
transplanted us into your land.
⁹ You cleared the ground for us,
and we took root and filled the land.
¹⁰ Our shade covered the mountains;
our branches covered the mighty cedars.
¹¹ We spread our branches west to the
Mediterranean Sea;
our shoots spread east to the Euphrates
River.*
¹² But now, why have you broken down our
walls
so that all who pass by may steal our
fruit?
¹³ The wild boar from the forest devours it,
and the wild animals feed on it.

¹⁴ Come back, we beg you, O God of Heaven's
Armies.
Look down from heaven and see our
plight.
Take care of this grapevine
¹⁵ that you yourself have planted,
this son you have raised for yourself.
¹⁶ For we are chopped up and burned by our
enemies.
May they perish at the sight of your frown.
¹⁷ Strengthen the man you love,
the son of your choice.
¹⁸ Then we will never abandon you again.
Revive us so we can call on your name
once more.

¹⁹ Turn us again to yourself, O LORD God of
Heaven's Armies.
Make your face shine down upon us.
Only then will we be saved.

81 *For the choir director: A psalm
of Asaph, to be accompanied by
a stringed instrument.**

¹ Sing praises to God, our strength.
Sing to the God of Jacob.
² Sing! Beat the tambourine.
Play the sweet lyre and the harp.
³ Blow the ram's horn at new moon,
and again at full moon to call a festival!
⁴ For this is required by the decrees of
Israel;
it is a regulation of the God of Jacob.

⁵ He made it a law for Israel*
when he attacked Egypt to set us free.

I heard an unknown voice say,
⁶ "Now I will take the load from your
shoulders;
I will free your hands from their heavy
tasks.
⁷ You cried to me in trouble, and I saved
you;
I answered out of the thundercloud
and tested your faith when there was no
water at Meribah.   *Interlude*

⁸ "Listen to me, O my people, while I give
you stern warnings.
O Israel, if you would only listen to me!
⁹ You must never have a foreign god;
you must not bow down before a false
god.
¹⁰ For it was I, the LORD your God,
who rescued you from the land of
Egypt.
Open your mouth wide, and I will fill it
with good things.

¹¹ "But no, my people wouldn't listen.
Israel did not want me around.
¹² So I let them follow their own stubborn
desires,
living according to their own ideas.
¹³ Oh, that my people would listen to me!
Oh, that Israel would follow me,
walking in my paths!
¹⁴ How quickly I would then subdue their
enemies!
How soon my hands would be upon
their foes!
¹⁵ Those who hate the LORD would cringe
before him;
they would be doomed forever.
¹⁶ But I would feed you with the finest wheat.
I would satisfy you with wild honey
from the rock."

82 *A psalm of Asaph.*

¹ God presides over heaven's court;
he pronounces judgment on the
heavenly beings:
² "How long will you hand down unjust
decisions
by favoring the wicked?   *Interlude*

³ "Give justice to the poor and the orphan;
uphold the rights of the oppressed and
the destitute.

⁴ Rescue the poor and helpless;
    deliver them from the grasp of evil
    people.
⁵ But these oppressors know nothing;
    they are so ignorant!
They wander about in darkness,
    while the whole world is shaken to the
    core.
⁶ I say, 'You are gods;
    you are all children of the Most High.
⁷ But you will die like mere mortals
    and fall like every other ruler.'"

⁸ Rise up, O God, and judge the earth,
    for all the nations belong to you.

83 A song. A psalm of Asaph.

¹ O God, do not be silent!
    Do not be deaf.
    Do not be quiet, O God.
² Don't you hear the uproar of your enemies?
    Don't you see that your arrogant
    enemies are rising up?
³ They devise crafty schemes against your
    people;
    they conspire against your precious ones.
⁴ "Come," they say, "let us wipe out Israel
    as a nation.
    We will destroy the very memory of its
    existence."
⁵ Yes, this was their unanimous decision.
    They signed a treaty as allies against
    you—
⁶ these Edomites and Ishmaelites;
    Moabites and Hagrites;
⁷ Gebalites, Ammonites, and Amalekites;
    and people from Philistia and Tyre.
⁸ Assyria has joined them, too,
    and is allied with the descendants of
    Lot.   *Interlude*

⁹ Do to them as you did to the Midianites
    and as you did to Sisera and Jabin at the
    Kishon River.
¹⁰ They were destroyed at Endor,
    and their decaying corpses fertilized the
    soil.
¹¹ Let their mighty nobles die as Oreb and
    Zeeb did.
    Let all their princes die like Zebah and
    Zalmunna.
¹² for they said, "Let us seize for our own use
    these pasturelands of God!"
¹³ O my God, scatter them like tumbleweed,
    like chaff before the wind!

¹⁴ As a fire burns a forest
    and as a flame sets mountains ablaze,
¹⁵ chase them with your fierce storm;
    terrify them with your tempest.
¹⁶ Utterly disgrace them
    until they submit to your name, O LORD.
¹⁷ Let them be ashamed and terrified forever.
    Let them die in disgrace.
¹⁸ Then they will learn that you alone are
    called the LORD,
    that you alone are the Most High,
    supreme over all the earth.

84 For the choir director: A psalm of the descendants of Korah, to be accompanied by a stringed instrument.*

¹ How lovely is your dwelling place,
    O LORD of Heaven's Armies.
² I long, yes, I faint with longing
    to enter the courts of the LORD.
With my whole being, body and soul,
    I will shout joyfully to the living God.
³ Even the sparrow finds a home,
    and the swallow builds her nest and
    raises her young
at a place near your altar,
    O LORD of Heaven's Armies, my King
    and my God!
⁴ What joy for those who can live in your
    house,
    always singing your praises.   *Interlude*

⁵ What joy for those whose strength comes
    from the LORD,
    who have set their minds on a
    pilgrimage to Jerusalem.
⁶ When they walk through the Valley of
    Weeping,*
    it will become a place of refreshing
    springs.
    The autumn rains will clothe it with
    blessings.
⁷ They will continue to grow stronger,
    and each of them will appear before God
    in Jerusalem.*

⁸ O LORD God of Heaven's Armies, hear my
    prayer.
    Listen, O God of Jacob.   *Interlude*

⁹ O God, look with favor upon the king, our
    shield!
    Show favor to the one you have
    anointed.

80:11 Hebrew *west to the sea, . . . east to the river.* **81:**TITLE Hebrew *according to the gittith.* **81:5** Hebrew *for Joseph.* **84:**TITLE Hebrew *according to the gittith.* **84:6** Or *Valley of Poplars;* Hebrew reads *valley of Baca.* **84:7** Hebrew *Zion.*

¹⁰ A single day in your courts
    is better than a thousand anywhere else!
I would rather be a gatekeeper in the
        house of my God
    than live the good life in the homes of
        the wicked.
¹¹ For the LORD God is our sun and our
        shield.
    He gives us grace and glory.
    The LORD will withhold no good thing
        from those who do what is right.
¹² O LORD of Heaven's Armies,
    what joy for those who trust in you.

85 *For the choir director: A psalm of the descendants of Korah.*

¹ LORD, you poured out blessings on your
        land!
    You restored the fortunes of Israel.*
² You forgave the guilt of your people—
    yes, you covered all their sins. *Interlude*
³ You held back your fury.
    You kept back your blazing anger.

⁴ Now restore us again, O God of our
        salvation.
    Put aside your anger against us once
        more.
⁵ Will you be angry with us always?
    Will you prolong your wrath to all
        generations?
⁶ Won't you revive us again,
    so your people can rejoice in you?
⁷ Show us your unfailing love, O LORD,
    and grant us your salvation.

⁸ I listen carefully to what God the LORD is
        saying,
    for he speaks peace to his faithful
        people.
    But let them not return to their foolish
        ways.
⁹ Surely his salvation is near to those who
        fear him,
    so our land will be filled with his glory.

¹⁰ Unfailing love and truth have met
        together.
    Righteousness and peace have kissed!
¹¹ Truth springs up from the earth,
    and righteousness smiles down from
        heaven.
¹² Yes, the LORD pours down his blessings.
    Our land will yield its bountiful harvest.
¹³ Righteousness goes as a herald before
        him,
    preparing the way for his steps.

86 *A prayer of David.*

¹ Bend down, O LORD, and hear my prayer;
    answer me, for I need your help.
² Protect me, for I am devoted to you.
    Save me, for I serve you and trust you.
    You are my God.
³ Be merciful to me, O Lord,
    for I am calling on you constantly.
⁴ Give me happiness, O Lord,
    for I give myself to you.
⁵ O Lord, you are so good, so ready to
        forgive,
    so full of unfailing love for all who ask
        for your help.
⁶ Listen closely to my prayer, O LORD;
    hear my urgent cry.
⁷ I will call to you whenever I'm in trouble,
    and you will answer me.

⁸ No pagan god is like you, O Lord.
    None can do what you do!
⁹ All the nations you made
    will come and bow before you, Lord;
    they will praise your holy name.
¹⁰ For you are great and perform wonderful
        deeds.
    You alone are God.

¹¹ Teach me your ways, O LORD,
    that I may live according to your truth!
Grant me purity of heart,
    so that I may honor you.
¹² With all my heart I will praise you, O Lord
        my God.
    I will give glory to your name forever,
¹³ for your love for me is very great.
    You have rescued me from the depths of
        death.*

¹⁴ O God, insolent people rise up against me;
    a violent gang is trying to kill me.
    You mean nothing to them.
¹⁵ But you, O Lord,
    are a God of compassion and mercy,
slow to get angry
    and filled with unfailing love and
        faithfulness.
¹⁶ Look down and have mercy on me.
    Give your strength to your servant;
    save me, the son of your servant.
¹⁷ Send me a sign of your favor.
    Then those who hate me will be put to
        shame,
    for you, O LORD, help and comfort me.

Lost Prayers

OUR DAILY BREAD PSALM 86

The headline read: UNANSWERED PRAYERS: LETTERS TO GOD FOUND DUMPED IN OCEAN.

The letters, three hundred in all and sent to a New Jersey minister, had been tossed in the ocean, most of them unopened. The minister was long dead. How the letters came to be floating in the surf off the New Jersey shore is a mystery.

The letters were addressed to the minister because he had promised to pray. Some of the letters asked for frivolous things; others were written by anguished spouses, children, or widows. They poured out their hearts to God, asking for help with relatives who were abusing drugs and alcohol, or spouses who were cheating on them. One asked God for a husband and father to love her child. The reporter concluded that all were "unanswered prayers."

> I will call to you whenever I'm in trouble, and you will answer me.
>
> PSALM 86:7

Not so! If those letter-writers cried out to God, He heard each one of them. Not one honest prayer is lost to His ears. "You know what I long for, Lord," David wrote in the midst of a deep personal crisis, "you hear my every sigh" (Ps 38:9). David understood that we can cast all our cares on the Lord, even if no one else prays for us. He confidently concluded, "I will call to you whenever I'm in trouble, and you will answer me" (86:7). —DHR

Lord, you hear my every prayer, even my thoughts that I can't put into words. Thank you for always hearing my prayers and answering them as you know is for my good.

Jesus hears our faintest cry.

DAY 14: pg 61

87 *A song. A psalm of the descendants of Korah.*

¹ On the holy mountain
  stands the city founded by the LORD.
² He loves the city of Jerusalem
  more than any other city in Israel.*
³ O city of God,
  what glorious things are said of you!
                            Interlude

⁴ I will count Egypt* and Babylon among
    those who know me—
  also Philistia and Tyre, and even distant
    Ethiopia.*
  They have all become citizens of
    Jerusalem!

⁵ Regarding Jerusalem* it will be said,
    "Everyone enjoys the rights of
    citizenship there."
  And the Most High will personally bless
    this city.
⁶ When the LORD registers the nations, he
    will say,
  "They have all become citizens of
    Jerusalem."   *Interlude*

⁷ The people will play flutes* and sing,
    "The source of my life springs from
    Jerusalem!"

85:1 Hebrew *of Jacob.* See note on 44:4. 86:13 Hebrew *of Sheol.*
87:2 Hebrew *He loves the gates of Zion more than all the dwellings of Jacob.* See note on 44:4. 87:4a Hebrew *Rahab,* the name of a mythical sea monster that represents chaos in ancient literature. The name is used here as a poetic name for Egypt. 87:4b Hebrew *Cush.*
87:5 Hebrew *Zion.* 87:7 Or *will dance.*

88

For the choir director: A psalm of the descendants of Korah. A song to be sung to the tune "The Suffering of Affliction." A psalm* of Heman the Ezrahite.

¹ O LORD, God of my salvation,
    I cry out to you by day.
    I come to you at night.
² Now hear my prayer;
    listen to my cry.
³ For my life is full of troubles,
    and death* draws near.
⁴ I am as good as dead,
    like a strong man with no strength
        left.
⁵ They have left me among the dead,
    and I lie like a corpse in a grave.
I am forgotten,
    cut off from your care.
⁶ You have thrown me into the lowest pit,
    into the darkest depths.
⁷ Your anger weighs me down;
    with wave after wave you have
        engulfed me.   *Interlude*

⁸ You have driven my friends away
    by making me repulsive to them.
I am in a trap with no way of escape.
⁹   My eyes are blinded by my tears.
Each day I beg for your help, O LORD;
    I lift my hands to you for mercy.
¹⁰ Are your wonderful deeds of any use to the
        dead?
    Do the dead rise up and praise you?
                        Interlude

¹¹ Can those in the grave declare your
        unfailing love?
    Can they proclaim your faithfulness in
        the place of destruction?*
¹² Can the darkness speak of your wonderful
        deeds?
    Can anyone in the land of forgetfulness
        talk about your righteousness?
¹³ O LORD, I cry out to you.
    I will keep on pleading day by day.
¹⁴ O LORD, why do you reject me?
    Why do you turn your face from me?

¹⁵ I have been sick and close to death since
        my youth.
    I stand helpless and desperate before
        your terrors.
¹⁶ Your fierce anger has overwhelmed me.
    Your terrors have paralyzed me.
¹⁷ They swirl around me like floodwaters all
        day long.
    They have engulfed me completely.

¹⁸ You have taken away my companions and
        loved ones.
    Darkness is my closest friend.

89

A psalm* of Ethan the Ezrahite.

¹ I will sing of the LORD's unfailing love
        forever!
    Young and old will hear of your
        faithfulness.
² Your unfailing love will last forever.
    Your faithfulness is as enduring as the
        heavens.

³ The LORD said, "I have made a covenant
        with David, my chosen servant.
    I have sworn this oath to him:
⁴ 'I will establish your descendants as kings
        forever;
    they will sit on your throne from now
        until eternity.'"   *Interlude*
⁵ All heaven will praise your great wonders,
        LORD;
    myriads of angels will praise you for
        your faithfulness.
⁶ For who in all of heaven can compare with
        the LORD?
    What mightiest angel is anything like
        the LORD?
⁷ The highest angelic powers stand in awe
        of God.
    He is far more awesome than all who
        surround his throne.
⁸ O LORD God of Heaven's Armies!
    Where is there anyone as mighty as you,
        O LORD?
    You are entirely faithful.

⁹ You rule the oceans.
    You subdue their storm-tossed waves.
¹⁰ You crushed the great sea monster.*
    You scattered your enemies with your
        mighty arm.
¹¹ The heavens are yours, and the earth is
        yours;
    everything in the world is yours—you
        created it all.
¹² You created north and south.
    Mount Tabor and Mount Hermon praise
        your name.
¹³ Powerful is your arm!
    Strong is your hand!
    Your right hand is lifted high in glorious
        strength.
¹⁴ Righteousness and justice are the
        foundation of your throne.
    Unfailing love and truth walk before you
        as attendants.

¹⁵ Happy are those who hear the joyful call
    to worship,
    for they will walk in the light of your
    presence, LORD.
¹⁶ They rejoice all day long in your wonderful
    reputation.
    They exult in your righteousness.
¹⁷ You are their glorious strength.
    It pleases you to make us strong.
¹⁸ Yes, our protection comes from the LORD,
    and he, the Holy One of Israel, has given
    us our king.

¹⁹ Long ago you spoke in a vision to your
    faithful people.
    You said, "I have raised up a warrior.
    I have selected him from the common
    people to be king.
²⁰ I have found my servant David.
    I have anointed him with my holy oil.
²¹ I will steady him with my hand;
    with my powerful arm I will make him
    strong.
²² His enemies will not defeat him,
    nor will the wicked overpower him.
²³ I will beat down his adversaries before
    him
    and destroy those who hate him.
²⁴ My faithfulness and unfailing love will be
    with him,
    and by my authority he will grow in
    power.
²⁵ I will extend his rule over the sea,
    his dominion over the rivers.
²⁶ And he will call out to me, 'You are my
    Father,
    my God, and the Rock of my salvation.'
²⁷ I will make him my firstborn son,
    the mightiest king on earth.
²⁸ I will love him and be kind to him
    forever;
    my covenant with him will never end.
²⁹ I will preserve an heir for him;
    his throne will be as endless as the days
    of heaven.
³⁰ But if his descendants forsake my
    instructions
    and fail to obey my regulations,
³¹ if they do not obey my decrees
    and fail to keep my commands,
³² then I will punish their sin with the rod,
    and their disobedience with beating.
³³ But I will never stop loving him
    nor fail to keep my promise to him.
³⁴ No, I will not break my covenant;
    I will not take back a single word I said.

³⁵ I have sworn an oath to David,
    and in my holiness I cannot lie:
³⁶ His dynasty will go on forever;
    his kingdom will endure as the sun.
³⁷ It will be as eternal as the moon,
    my faithful witness in the sky!"
                                            Interlude

³⁸ But now you have rejected him and cast
    him off.
    You are angry with your anointed king.
³⁹ You have renounced your covenant with
    him;
    you have thrown his crown in the dust.
⁴⁰ You have broken down the walls
    protecting him
    and ruined every fort defending him.
⁴¹ Everyone who comes along has robbed
    him,
    and he has become a joke to his
    neighbors.
⁴² You have strengthened his enemies
    and made them all rejoice.
⁴³ You have made his sword useless
    and refused to help him in battle.
⁴⁴ You have ended his splendor
    and overturned his throne.
⁴⁵ You have made him old before his time
    and publicly disgraced him.   *Interlude*

⁴⁶ O LORD, how long will this go on?
    Will you hide yourself forever?
    How long will your anger burn like
    fire?
⁴⁷ Remember how short my life is,
    how empty and futile this human
    existence!
⁴⁸ No one can live forever; all will die.
    No one can escape the power of the
    grave.*   *Interlude*

⁴⁹ Lord, where is your unfailing love?
    You promised it to David with a faithful
    pledge.
⁵⁰ Consider, Lord, how your servants are
    disgraced!
    I carry in my heart the insults of so
    many people.
⁵¹ Your enemies have mocked me, O LORD;
    they mock your anointed king wherever
    he goes.

⁵² Praise the LORD forever!
    Amen and amen!

88:TITLE Hebrew *maskil*. This may be a literary or musical term.
88:3 Hebrew *Sheol*. 88:11 Hebrew *in Abaddon?* 89:TITLE Hebrew
maskil. This may be a literary or musical term. 89:10 Hebrew *Rahab*,
the name of a mythical sea monster that represents chaos in ancient
literature. 89:48 Hebrew *of Sheol*.

BOOK FOUR (Psalms 90–106)

90 *A prayer of Moses, the man of God.*

1 Lord, through all the generations
  you have been our home!
2 Before the mountains were born,
    before you gave birth to the earth and
      the world,
    from beginning to end, you are God.

3 You turn people back to dust, saying,
    "Return to dust, you mortals!"
4 For you, a thousand years are as a passing
      day,
    as brief as a few night hours.
5 You sweep people away like dreams that
      disappear.
    They are like grass that springs up in the
      morning.
6 In the morning it blooms and flourishes,
    but by evening it is dry and withered.
7 We wither beneath your anger;
    we are overwhelmed by your fury.
8 You spread out our sins before you—
    our secret sins—and you see them all.
9 We live our lives beneath your wrath,
    ending our years with a groan.

10 Seventy years are given to us!
    Some even live to eighty.
  But even the best years are filled with pain
      and trouble;
    soon they disappear, and we fly away.
11 Who can comprehend the power of your
      anger?
    Your wrath is as awesome as the fear
      you deserve.
12 Teach us to realize the brevity of life,
    so that we may grow in wisdom.

13 O LORD, come back to us!
    How long will you delay?
    Take pity on your servants!
14 Satisfy us each morning with your
      unfailing love,
    so we may sing for joy to the end of our
      lives.
15 Give us gladness in proportion to our
      former misery!
    Replace the evil years with good.
16 Let us, your servants, see you work
      again;
    let our children see your glory.
17 And may the Lord our God show us his
      approval
    and make our efforts successful.
    Yes, make our efforts successful!

91
1 Those who live in the shelter of the
      Most High
    will find rest in the shadow of the
      Almighty.
2 This I declare about the LORD:
    He alone is my refuge, my place of safety;
    he is my God, and I trust him.
3 For he will rescue you from every trap
    and protect you from deadly disease.
4 He will cover you with his feathers.
    He will shelter you with his wings.
    His faithful promises are your armor
      and protection.
5 Do not be afraid of the terrors of the
      night,
    nor the arrow that flies in the day.
6 Do not dread the disease that stalks in
      darkness,
    nor the disaster that strikes at midday.
7 Though a thousand fall at your side,
    though ten thousand are dying around
      you,
    these evils will not touch you.
8 Just open your eyes,
    and see how the wicked are punished.

9 If you make the LORD your refuge,
    if you make the Most High your shelter,
10 no evil will conquer you;
    no plague will come near your home.
11 For he will order his angels
    to protect you wherever you go.
12 They will hold you up with their hands
    so you won't even hurt your foot on a
      stone.
13 You will trample upon lions and cobras;
    you will crush fierce lions and serpents
      under your feet!

14 The LORD says, "I will rescue those who
      love me.
    I will protect those who trust in my
      name.
15 When they call on me, I will answer;
    I will be with them in trouble.
    I will rescue and honor them.
16 I will reward them with a long life
    and give them my salvation."

92 *A psalm. A song to be sung on the Sabbath Day.*

1 It is good to give thanks to the LORD,
    to sing praises to the Most High.
2 It is good to proclaim your unfailing love
      in the morning,
    your faithfulness in the evening,

³ accompanied by the ten-stringed harp
and the melody of the lyre.

⁴ You thrill me, LORD, with all you have
done for me!
I sing for joy because of what you have
done.
⁵ O LORD, what great works you do!
And how deep are your thoughts.
⁶ Only a simpleton would not know,
and only a fool would not understand
this:
⁷ Though the wicked sprout like weeds
and evildoers flourish,
they will be destroyed forever.

⁸ But you, O LORD, will be exalted
forever.
⁹ Your enemies, LORD, will surely perish;
all evildoers will be scattered.
¹⁰ But you have made me as strong as a
wild ox.
You have anointed me with the
finest oil.
¹¹ My eyes have seen the downfall of my
enemies;
my ears have heard the defeat of my
wicked opponents.
¹² But the godly will flourish like palm
trees
and grow strong like the cedars of
Lebanon.
¹³ For they are transplanted to the LORD's
own house.
They flourish in the courts of our God.
¹⁴ Even in old age they will still produce
fruit;
they will remain vital and green.
¹⁵ They will declare, "The LORD is just!
He is my rock!
There is no evil in him!"

93 ¹ The LORD is king! He is robed in
majesty.
Indeed, the LORD is robed in majesty
and armed with strength.
The world stands firm
and cannot be shaken.

² Your throne, O LORD, has stood from time
immemorial.
You yourself are from the everlasting
past.
³ The floods have risen up, O LORD.
The floods have roared like thunder;
the floods have lifted their pounding
waves.

⁴ But mightier than the violent raging of the
seas,
mightier than the breakers on the
shore—
the LORD above is mightier than these!
⁵ Your royal laws cannot be changed.
Your reign, O LORD, is holy forever and
ever.

94 ¹ O LORD, the God of vengeance,
O God of vengeance, let your
glorious justice shine forth!
² Arise, O judge of the earth.
Give the proud what they deserve.
³ How long, O LORD?
How long will the wicked be allowed to
gloat?
⁴ How long will they speak with arrogance?
How long will these evil people boast?
⁵ They crush your people, LORD,
hurting those you claim as your own.
⁶ They kill widows and foreigners
and murder orphans.
⁷ "The LORD isn't looking," they say,
"and besides, the God of Israel* doesn't
care."

⁸ Think again, you fools!
When will you finally catch on?
⁹ Is he deaf—the one who made your ears?
Is he blind—the one who formed your
eyes?
¹⁰ He punishes the nations—won't he also
punish you?
He knows everything—doesn't he also
know what you are doing?
¹¹ The LORD knows people's thoughts;
he knows they are worthless!

¹² Joyful are those you discipline, LORD,
those you teach with your instructions.
¹³ You give them relief from troubled times
until a pit is dug to capture the wicked.
¹⁴ The LORD will not reject his people;
he will not abandon his special
possession.
¹⁵ Judgment will again be founded on
justice,
and those with virtuous hearts will
pursue it.

¹⁶ Who will protect me from the wicked?
Who will stand up for me against
evildoers?
¹⁷ Unless the LORD had helped me,
I would soon have settled in the silence
of the grave.

94:7 Hebrew *of Jacob*. See note on 44:4.

¹⁸ I cried out, "I am slipping!"
 but your unfailing love, O LORD,
  supported me.
¹⁹ When doubts filled my mind,
 your comfort gave me renewed hope
  and cheer.

²⁰ Can unjust leaders claim that God is on
  their side—
 leaders whose decrees permit injustice?
²¹ They gang up against the righteous
 and condemn the innocent to death.
²² But the LORD is my fortress;
 my God is the mighty rock where I hide.
²³ God will turn the sins of evil people back
  on them.
 He will destroy them for their sins.
 The LORD our God will destroy them.

95

¹ Come, let us sing to the LORD!
 Let us shout joyfully to the Rock of
  our salvation.
² Let us come to him with thanksgiving.
 Let us sing psalms of praise to him.
³ For the LORD is a great God,
 a great King above all gods.
⁴ He holds in his hands the depths of the
  earth
 and the mightiest mountains.
⁵ The sea belongs to him, for he made it.
 His hands formed the dry land, too.

⁶ Come, let us worship and bow down.
 Let us kneel before the LORD our
  maker,
⁷ for he is our God.
 We are the people he watches over,
 the flock under his care.

If only you would listen to his voice today!
⁸ The LORD says, "Don't harden your hearts
  as Israel did at Meribah,
 as they did at Massah in the wilderness.
⁹ For there your ancestors tested and tried
  my patience,
 even though they saw everything I did.
¹⁰ For forty years I was angry with them, and
  I said,
 'They are a people whose hearts turn away
  from me.
 They refuse to do what I tell them.'
¹¹ So in my anger I took an oath:
 'They will never enter my place of rest.'"

96

¹ Sing a new song to the LORD!
 Let the whole earth sing to the
  LORD!

² Sing to the LORD; praise his name.
 Each day proclaim the good news that
  he saves.
³ Publish his glorious deeds among the
  nations.
 Tell everyone about the amazing things
  he does.
⁴ Great is the LORD! He is most worthy of
  praise!
 He is to be feared above all gods.
⁵ The gods of other nations are mere idols,
 but the LORD made the heavens!
⁶ Honor and majesty surround him;
 strength and beauty fill his sanctuary.

⁷ O nations of the world, recognize the
  LORD;
 recognize that the LORD is glorious and
  strong.
⁸ Give to the LORD the glory he deserves!
 Bring your offering and come into his
  courts.
⁹ Worship the LORD in all his holy splendor.
 Let all the earth tremble before him.
¹⁰ Tell all the nations, "The LORD reigns!"
 The world stands firm and cannot be
  shaken.
 He will judge all peoples fairly.

¹¹ Let the heavens be glad, and the earth
  rejoice!
 Let the sea and everything in it shout
  his praise!
¹² Let the fields and their crops burst out
  with joy!
 Let the trees of the forest rustle with
  praise
¹³ before the LORD, for he is coming!
 He is coming to judge the earth.
 He will judge the world with justice,
 and the nations with his truth.

97

¹ The LORD is king!
 Let the earth rejoice!
 Let the farthest coastlands be glad.
² Dark clouds surround him.
 Righteousness and justice are the
  foundation of his throne.
³ Fire spreads ahead of him
 and burns up all his foes.
⁴ His lightning flashes out across the world.
 The earth sees and trembles.
⁵ The mountains melt like wax before the
  LORD,
 before the Lord of all the earth.
⁶ The heavens proclaim his righteousness;
 every nation sees his glory.

Mightier Than All

OUR DAILY BREAD PSALM 93

Iguazu Falls on the border of Brazil and Argentina is a spectacular waterfall system of 275 falls along 2.7 km (1.67 miles) of the Iguazu River. Etched on a wall on the Brazilian side of the Falls are the words of Psalm 93:4, "Mightier than the thunders of many waters, mightier than the waves of the sea, the LORD on high is mighty!" (RSV). Below it are these words, "God is always greater than all of our troubles."

The writer of Psalm 93, who penned its words during the time that kings reigned, knew that God is the ultimate King over all. "The LORD is king!" he wrote. "Your throne, O LORD, has stood from time immemorial. You yourself are from the everlasting past" (vv. 1–2). No matter how high the floods or waves, the Lord remains greater than them all.

The roar of a waterfall is truly majestic, but it is quite a different matter to be in the water hurtling toward the falls. That may be the situation you are in today. Physical, financial, or relational problems loom ever larger and you feel like you are about to go over the falls. In such situations, the Christian has Someone to turn to. He is the Lord, "who is able, through his mighty power at work within us, to accomplish infinitely more than we might ask or think" (Eph 3:20). Our God is greater than all of our troubles. —HCP

> The LORD is king! He is robed in majesty. Indeed, the LORD is robed in majesty and armed with strength. The world stands firm and cannot be shaken.
>
> PSALM 93:1

Lord, even when it seems as if I'm being carried along by a mighty wave that's destroying everything in its wake, I can rest in the assurance that you are so much mightier and that you care for me. I stand secure in your strength, because you are the Rock.

Never measure God's unlimited power by your limited expectations.

DAY 15: pg 63

7 Those who worship idols are disgraced—
   all who brag about their worthless gods—
   for every god must bow to him.
8 Jerusalem* has heard and rejoiced,
   and all the towns of Judah are glad
   because of your justice, O LORD!
9 For you, O LORD, are supreme over all the earth;
   you are exalted far above all gods.

10 You who love the LORD, hate evil!
   He protects the lives of his godly people
   and rescues them from the power of the wicked.

11 Light shines on the godly,
   and joy on those whose hearts are right.
12 May all who are godly rejoice in the LORD
   and praise his holy name!

98 *A psalm.*

1 Sing a new song to the LORD,
   for he has done wonderful deeds.
   His right hand has won a mighty victory;
   his holy arm has shown his saving power!

97:8 Hebrew *Zion.*

² The LORD has announced his victory
and has revealed his righteousness to
every nation!
³ He has remembered his promise to love
and be faithful to Israel.
The ends of the earth have seen the
victory of our God.

⁴ Shout to the LORD, all the earth;
break out in praise and sing for joy!
⁵ Sing your praise to the LORD with the
harp,
with the harp and melodious song,
⁶ with trumpets and the sound of the ram's
horn.
Make a joyful symphony before the
LORD, the King!

⁷ Let the sea and everything in it shout his
praise!
Let the earth and all living things join in.
⁸ Let the rivers clap their hands in glee!
Let the hills sing out their songs of joy
⁹ before the LORD.
For the LORD is coming to judge the
earth.
He will judge the world with justice,
and the nations with fairness.

99
¹ The LORD is king!
Let the nations tremble!
He sits on his throne between the
cherubim.
Let the whole earth quake!
² The LORD sits in majesty in Jerusalem,*
exalted above all the nations.
³ Let them praise your great and awesome
name.
Your name is holy!
⁴ Mighty King, lover of justice,
you have established fairness.
You have acted with justice
and righteousness throughout Israel.*
⁵ Exalt the LORD our God!
Bow low before his feet, for he is holy!

⁶ Moses and Aaron were among his priests;
Samuel also called on his name.
They cried to the LORD for help,
and he answered them.
⁷ He spoke to Israel from the pillar of cloud,
and they followed the laws and decrees
he gave them.
⁸ O LORD our God, you answered them.
You were a forgiving God to them,
but you punished them when they went
wrong.

⁹ Exalt the LORD our God,
and worship at his holy mountain in
Jerusalem,
for the LORD our God is holy!

100 *A psalm of thanksgiving.*

¹ Shout with joy to the LORD, all the earth!
² Worship the LORD with gladness.
Come before him, singing with joy.
³ Acknowledge that the LORD is God!
He made us, and we are his.*
We are his people, the sheep of his
pasture.
⁴ Enter his gates with thanksgiving;
go into his courts with praise.
Give thanks to him and praise his name.
⁵ For the LORD is good.
His unfailing love continues forever,
and his faithfulness continues to each
generation.

101 *A psalm of David.*

¹ I will sing of your love and justice, LORD.
I will praise you with songs.
² I will be careful to live a blameless life—
when will you come to help me?
I will lead a life of integrity
in my own home.
³ I will refuse to look at
anything vile and vulgar.
I hate all who deal crookedly;
I will have nothing to do with them.
⁴ I will reject perverse ideas
and stay away from every evil.
⁵ I will not tolerate people who slander their
neighbors.
I will not endure conceit and pride.

⁶ I will search for faithful people
to be my companions.
Only those who are above reproach
will be allowed to serve me.
⁷ I will not allow deceivers to serve in my
house,
and liars will not stay in my presence.
⁸ My daily task will be to ferret out the
wicked
and free the city of the LORD from their
grip.

102 *A prayer of one overwhelmed
with trouble, pouring out problems
before the LORD.*

¹ LORD, hear my prayer!
Listen to my plea!

Integrity 101

OUR DAILY BREAD PSALM 101

Officials in Philadelphia were astonished to receive a letter and payment from a motorist who had been given a speeding ticket in 1954. John, an English tourist, had been visiting the City of Brotherly Love when he was cited for speeding. The penalty was $15, but the man forgot about the ticket for almost fifty-two years until he discovered it in an old coat. "I thought, I've got to pay it," said John, 84, who now lives in a nursing home in East Sussex. "Englishmen pay their debts. My conscience is clear."

This story reminded me of the psalmist David's commitment to integrity. Although he made some terrible choices in his life, Psalm 101 declares his resolve to live blamelessly. His integrity would begin in the privacy of his own house (v. 2) and extend to his choice of colleagues and friends (vv. 6–7). In sharp contrast to the corrupt lives of most kings of the ancient Near East, David's integrity led him to respect the life of his sworn enemy, King Saul (1 Sam 24:4–6; 26:8–9).

> I will be careful to live a blameless life.... I will lead a life of integrity in my own home.
>
> PSALM 101:2

As followers of Jesus, we are called to walk in integrity and to maintain a clear conscience. When we honor our commitments to God and to others, we will walk in fellowship with God. Our integrity will guide us (Prov 11:3) and help us walk securely (10:9). —MLW

Heavenly Father, examine my heart and show me my errors, and then remind me to walk with integrity and honesty in all of my dealings with others. Praise God for deliverance and hope—and for the freedom of integrity.

There is no better test of a man's integrity than his behavior when he is wrong.

DAY 16: pg 65

² Don't turn away from me
  in my time of distress.
Bend down to listen,
  and answer me quickly when I call to you.
³ For my days disappear like smoke,
  and my bones burn like red-hot coals.
⁴ My heart is sick, withered like grass,
  and I have lost my appetite.
⁵ Because of my groaning,
  I am reduced to skin and bones.
⁶ I am like an owl in the desert,
  like a little owl in a far-off wilderness.
⁷ I lie awake,
  lonely as a solitary bird on the roof.

⁸ My enemies taunt me day after day.
  They mock and curse me.
⁹ I eat ashes for food.
  My tears run down into my drink
¹⁰ because of your anger and wrath.
  For you have picked me up and thrown me out.
¹¹ My life passes as swiftly as the evening shadows.
  I am withering away like grass.

¹² But you, O LORD, will sit on your throne forever.
  Your fame will endure to every generation.

99:2 Hebrew *Zion.* 99:4 Hebrew *Jacob.* See note on 44:4. 100:3 As in an alternate reading in the Masoretic Text; the other alternate and some ancient versions read *and not we ourselves.*

¹³ You will arise and have mercy on
  Jerusalem*—
  and now is the time to pity her,
  now is the time you promised to help.
¹⁴ For your people love every stone in her
  walls
  and cherish even the dust in her streets.
¹⁵ Then the nations will tremble before the
  LORD.
  The kings of the earth will tremble
  before his glory.
¹⁶ For the LORD will rebuild Jerusalem.
  He will appear in his glory.
¹⁷ He will listen to the prayers of the
  destitute.
  He will not reject their pleas.

¹⁸ Let this be recorded for future generations,
  so that a people not yet born will praise
  the LORD.
¹⁹ Tell them the LORD looked down
  from his heavenly sanctuary.
  He looked down to earth from heaven
²⁰ to hear the groans of the prisoners,
  to release those condemned to die.
²¹ And so the LORD's fame will be celebrated
  in Zion,
  his praises in Jerusalem,
²² when multitudes gather together
  and kingdoms come to worship the
  LORD.

²³ He broke my strength in midlife,
  cutting short my days.
²⁴ But I cried to him, "O my God, who lives
  forever,
  don't take my life while I am so young!
²⁵ Long ago you laid the foundation of the
  earth
  and made the heavens with your hands.
²⁶ They will perish, but you remain forever;
  they will wear out like old clothing.
  You will change them like a garment
  and discard them.
²⁷ But you are always the same;
  you will live forever.
²⁸ The children of your people
  will live in security.
  Their children's children
  will thrive in your presence."

103 *A psalm of David.*

¹ Let all that I am praise the LORD;
  with my whole heart, I will praise his
  holy name.

² Let all that I am praise the LORD;
  may I never forget the good things he
  does for me.
³ He forgives all my sins
  and heals all my diseases.
⁴ He redeems me from death
  and crowns me with love and tender
  mercies.
⁵ He fills my life with good things.
  My youth is renewed like the eagle's!

⁶ The LORD gives righteousness
  and justice to all who are treated
  unfairly.

⁷ He revealed his character to Moses
  and his deeds to the people of Israel.
⁸ The LORD is compassionate and merciful,
  slow to get angry and filled with
  unfailing love.
⁹ He will not constantly accuse us,
  nor remain angry forever.
¹⁰ He does not punish us for all our sins;
  he does not deal harshly with us, as we
  deserve.
¹¹ For his unfailing love toward those who
  fear him
  is as great as the height of the heavens
  above the earth.
¹² He has removed our sins as far from us
  as the east is from the west.
¹³ The LORD is like a father to his children,
  tender and compassionate to those who
  fear him.
¹⁴ For he knows how weak we are;
  he remembers we are only dust.
¹⁵ Our days on earth are like grass;
  like wildflowers, we bloom and die.
¹⁶ The wind blows, and we are gone—
  as though we had never been here.
¹⁷ But the love of the LORD remains forever
  with those who fear him.
  His salvation extends to the children's
  children
¹⁸ of those who are faithful to his
  covenant,
  of those who obey his commandments!

¹⁹ The LORD has made the heavens his
  throne;
  from there he rules over everything.

²⁰ Praise the LORD, you angels,
  you mighty ones who carry out his
  plans,
  listening for each of his commands.
²¹ Yes, praise the LORD, you armies of angels
  who serve him and do his will!

The Overflow

OUR DAILY BREAD PSALM 103

Joyful shouts filtered into our house from outside and I wanted to know what was so wonderful out there. I peeked through the curtains and watched two young boys splashing in a thick stream of water that gushed from a fire hydrant.

The overflow reminded me of how God pours out blessings on His children, and how important it is to recognize that "my cup overflows with blessings" (Ps 23:5).

Although I know He has furnished countless good things for me, when the car blows a gasket, when the flu infects my family, and when relationships threaten to unravel, dissatisfaction threatens my view of God's blessings—they seem more like infrequent drips from a faucet rather than a flood of water from a hydrant!

> Let all that I am praise the LORD; may I never forget the good things he does for me.
>
> PSALM 103:2

Maybe that's why in Psalm 103 David reminds us to "never forget the good things" that God does for us (v. 2). And then, to help us, he lists a torrent of blessings for believers. He reminds us that God forgives all our sins, heals all our diseases, redeems our lives from death, and crowns us with love (vv. 3–4).

Today, let's take time to acknowledge God's abundance instead of overlooking the overflow of His blessings. —JBS

Lord, when you pour out your blessings, they overflow into our lives. Our hearts are filled with gratitude and joy for your provision and your love.

Adding up your blessings will multiply your joy.

DAY 17: pg 73

²² Praise the LORD, everything he has created,
everything in all his kingdom.

Let all that I am praise the LORD.

104 ¹ Let all that I am praise the LORD.

O LORD my God, how great you are!
You are robed with honor and majesty.
² You are dressed in a robe of light.
You stretch out the starry curtain of the heavens;
³ you lay out the rafters of your home in the rain clouds.
You make the clouds your chariot;
you ride upon the wings of the wind.

⁴ The winds are your messengers;
flames of fire are your servants.*

⁵ You placed the world on its foundation
so it would never be moved.
⁶ You clothed the earth with floods of water,
water that covered even the mountains.
⁷ At your command, the water fled;
at the sound of your thunder, it hurried away.
⁸ Mountains rose and valleys sank
to the levels you decreed.

102:13 Hebrew *Zion;* also in 102:16.   104:4 Greek version reads *He sends his angels like the winds, / his servants like flames of fire.* Compare Heb 1:7.

⁹ Then you set a firm boundary for the seas,
so they would never again cover the
earth.

¹⁰ You make springs pour water into the
ravines,
so streams gush down from the
mountains.

¹¹ They provide water for all the animals,
and the wild donkeys quench their
thirst.

¹² The birds nest beside the streams
and sing among the branches of the
trees.

¹³ You send rain on the mountains from your
heavenly home,
and you fill the earth with the fruit of
your labor.

¹⁴ You cause grass to grow for the livestock
and plants for people to use.
You allow them to produce food from the
earth—

¹⁵ wine to make them glad,
olive oil to soothe their skin,
and bread to give them strength.

¹⁶ The trees of the LORD are well cared for—
the cedars of Lebanon that he planted.

¹⁷ There the birds make their nests,
and the storks make their homes in the
cypresses.

¹⁸ High in the mountains live the wild goats,
and the rocks form a refuge for the
hyraxes.*

¹⁹ You made the moon to mark the seasons,
and the sun knows when to set.

²⁰ You send the darkness, and it becomes
night,
when all the forest animals prowl
about.

²¹ Then the young lions roar for their prey,
stalking the food provided by God.

²² At dawn they slink back
into their dens to rest.

²³ Then people go off to their work,
where they labor until evening.

²⁴ O LORD, what a variety of things you have
made!
In wisdom you have made them all.
The earth is full of your creatures.

²⁵ Here is the ocean, vast and wide,
teeming with life of every kind,
both large and small.

²⁶ See the ships sailing along,
and Leviathan,* which you made to play
in the sea.

²⁷ They all depend on you
to give them food as they need it.

²⁸ When you supply it, they gather it.
You open your hand to feed them,
and they are richly satisfied.

²⁹ But if you turn away from them, they
panic.
When you take away their breath,
they die and turn again to dust.

³⁰ When you give them your breath,* life is
created,
and you renew the face of the earth.

³¹ May the glory of the LORD continue
forever!
The LORD takes pleasure in all he has
made!

³² The earth trembles at his glance;
the mountains smoke at his touch.

³³ I will sing to the LORD as long as I live.
I will praise my God to my last breath!

³⁴ May all my thoughts be pleasing to him,
for I rejoice in the LORD.

³⁵ Let all sinners vanish from the face of the
earth;
let the wicked disappear forever.

Let all that I am praise the LORD.

Praise the LORD!

105 ¹ Give thanks to the LORD and
proclaim his greatness.
Let the whole world know what he has
done.

² Sing to him; yes, sing his praises.
Tell everyone about his wonderful
deeds.

³ Exult in his holy name;
rejoice, you who worship the LORD.

⁴ Search for the LORD and for his strength;
continually seek him.

⁵ Remember the wonders he has performed,
his miracles, and the rulings he has
given,

⁶ you children of his servant Abraham,
you descendants of Jacob, his chosen
ones.

⁷ He is the LORD our God.
His justice is seen throughout the land.

⁸ He always stands by his covenant—
the commitment he made to a thousand
generations.

⁹ This is the covenant he made with
Abraham
and the oath he swore to Isaac.

¹⁰ He confirmed it to Jacob as a decree,
  and to the people of Israel as a never-
  ending covenant:
¹¹ "I will give you the land of Canaan
  as your special possession."

¹² He said this when they were few in
  number,
  a tiny group of strangers in Canaan.
¹³ They wandered from nation to nation,
  from one kingdom to another.
¹⁴ Yet he did not let anyone oppress them.
  He warned kings on their behalf:
¹⁵ "Do not touch my chosen people,
  and do not hurt my prophets."

¹⁶ He called for a famine on the land of
  Canaan,
  cutting off its food supply.
¹⁷ Then he sent someone to Egypt ahead of
  them—
  Joseph, who was sold as a slave.
¹⁸ They bruised his feet with fetters
  and placed his neck in an iron collar.
¹⁹ Until the time came to fulfill his dreams,*
  the LORD tested Joseph's character.
²⁰ Then Pharaoh sent for him and set him
  free;
  the ruler of the nation opened his prison
  door.
²¹ Joseph was put in charge of all the king's
  household;
  he became ruler over all the king's
  possessions.
²² He could instruct the king's aides as he
  pleased
  and teach the king's advisers.

²³ Then Israel arrived in Egypt;
  Jacob lived as a foreigner in the land of
  Ham.
²⁴ And the LORD multiplied the people of
  Israel
  until they became too mighty for their
  enemies.
²⁵ Then he turned the Egyptians against the
  Israelites,
  and they plotted against the LORD's
  servants.

²⁶ But the LORD sent his servant Moses,
  along with Aaron, whom he had chosen.
²⁷ They performed miraculous signs among
  the Egyptians,
  and wonders in the land of Ham.
²⁸ The LORD blanketed Egypt in darkness,
  for they had defied his commands to let
  his people go.

²⁹ He turned their water into blood,
  poisoning all the fish.
³⁰ Then frogs overran the land
  and even invaded the king's bedrooms.
³¹ When the LORD spoke, flies descended on
  the Egyptians,
  and gnats swarmed across Egypt.
³² He sent them hail instead of rain,
  and lightning flashed over the land.
³³ He ruined their grapevines and fig trees
  and shattered all the trees.
³⁴ He spoke, and hordes of locusts came—
  young locusts beyond number.
³⁵ They ate up everything green in the land,
  destroying all the crops in their fields.
³⁶ Then he killed the oldest son in each
  Egyptian home,
  the pride and joy of each family.

³⁷ The LORD brought his people out of Egypt,
  loaded with silver and gold;
  and not one among the tribes of Israel
  even stumbled.
³⁸ Egypt was glad when they were gone,
  for they feared them greatly.
³⁹ The LORD spread a cloud above them as a
  covering
  and gave them a great fire to light the
  darkness.
⁴⁰ They asked for meat, and he sent them
  quail;
  he satisfied their hunger with manna—
  bread from heaven.
⁴¹ He split open a rock, and water gushed out
  to form a river through the dry
  wasteland.
⁴² For he remembered his sacred promise
  to his servant Abraham.
⁴³ So he brought his people out of Egypt with
  joy,
  his chosen ones with rejoicing.
⁴⁴ He gave his people the lands of pagan
  nations,
  and they harvested crops that others
  had planted.
⁴⁵ All this happened so they would follow his
  decrees
  and obey his instructions.

Praise the LORD!

106

¹ Praise the LORD!

  Give thanks to the LORD, for he is
  good!
  His faithful love endures forever.

104:18 Or *coneys,* or *rock badgers.* **104:26** The identification of
Leviathan is disputed, ranging from an earthly creature to a mythical
sea monster in ancient literature. **104:30** Or *When you send your Spirit.*
105:19 Hebrew *his word.*

2 Who can list the glorious miracles of the
 LORD?
 Who can ever praise him enough?
3 There is joy for those who deal justly with
 others
 and always do what is right.

4 Remember me, LORD, when you show
 favor to your people;
 come near and rescue me.
5 Let me share in the prosperity of your
 chosen ones.
 Let me rejoice in the joy of your people;
 let me praise you with those who are
 your heritage.

6 Like our ancestors, we have sinned.
 We have done wrong! We have acted
 wickedly!
7 Our ancestors in Egypt
 were not impressed by the LORD's
 miraculous deeds.
 They soon forgot his many acts of
 kindness to them.
 Instead, they rebelled against him at the
 Red Sea.*
8 Even so, he saved them—
 to defend the honor of his name
 and to demonstrate his mighty power.
9 He commanded the Red Sea* to dry up.
 He led Israel across the sea as if it were
 a desert.
10 So he rescued them from their enemies
 and redeemed them from their foes.
11 Then the water returned and covered their
 enemies;
 not one of them survived.
12 Then his people believed his promises.
 Then they sang his praise.

13 Yet how quickly they forgot what he had
 done!
 They wouldn't wait for his counsel!
14 In the wilderness their desires ran wild,
 testing God's patience in that dry
 wasteland.
15 So he gave them what they asked for,
 but he sent a plague along with it.
16 The people in the camp were jealous of
 Moses
 and envious of Aaron, the LORD's holy
 priest.
17 Because of this, the earth opened up;
 it swallowed Dathan
 and buried Abiram and the other rebels.
18 Fire fell upon their followers;
 a flame consumed the wicked.

19 The people made a calf at Mount Sinai*;
 they bowed before an image made of
 gold.
20 They traded their glorious God
 for a statue of a grass-eating bull.
21 They forgot God, their savior,
 who had done such great things in
 Egypt—
22 such wonderful things in the land of
 Ham,
 such awesome deeds at the Red Sea.
23 So he declared he would destroy them.
 But Moses, his chosen one, stepped
 between the LORD and the people.
 He begged him to turn from his anger
 and not destroy them.

24 The people refused to enter the pleasant
 land,
 for they wouldn't believe his promise to
 care for them.
25 Instead, they grumbled in their tents
 and refused to obey the LORD.
26 Therefore, he solemnly swore
 that he would kill them in the
 wilderness,
27 that he would scatter their descendants
 among the nations,
 exiling them to distant lands.

28 Then our ancestors joined in the worship
 of Baal at Peor;
 they even ate sacrifices offered to the
 dead!
29 They angered the LORD with all these
 things,
 so a plague broke out among them.
30 But Phinehas had the courage to
 intervene,
 and the plague was stopped.
31 So he has been regarded as a righteous
 man
 ever since that time.

32 At Meribah, too, they angered the LORD,
 causing Moses serious trouble.
33 They made Moses angry,*
 and he spoke foolishly.

34 Israel failed to destroy the nations in the
 land,
 as the LORD had commanded them.
35 Instead, they mingled among the pagans
 and adopted their evil customs.
36 They worshiped their idols,
 which led to their downfall.
37 They even sacrificed their sons
 and their daughters to the demons.

³⁸ They shed innocent blood,
the blood of their sons and daughters.
By sacrificing them to the idols of Canaan,
they polluted the land with murder.
³⁹ They defiled themselves by their evil deeds,
and their love of idols was adultery in
the LORD's sight.

⁴⁰ That is why the LORD's anger burned
against his people,
and he abhorred his own special
possession.
⁴¹ He handed them over to pagan nations,
and they were ruled by those who hated
them.
⁴² Their enemies crushed them
and brought them under their cruel
power.
⁴³ Again and again he rescued them,
but they chose to rebel against him,
and they were finally destroyed by their
sin.
⁴⁴ Even so, he pitied them in their distress
and listened to their cries.
⁴⁵ He remembered his covenant with them
and relented because of his unfailing
love.
⁴⁶ He even caused their captors
to treat them with kindness.

⁴⁷ Save us, O LORD our God!
Gather us back from among the nations,
so we can thank your holy name
and rejoice and praise you.

⁴⁸ Praise the LORD, the God of Israel,
who lives from everlasting to
everlasting!
Let all the people say, "Amen!"

Praise the LORD!

BOOK FIVE (Psalms 107–150)

107

¹ Give thanks to the LORD, for he is
good!
His faithful love endures forever.
² Has the LORD redeemed you? Then speak
out!
Tell others he has redeemed you from
your enemies.
³ For he has gathered the exiles from many
lands,
from east and west,
from north and south.

⁴ Some wandered in the wilderness,
lost and homeless.
⁵ Hungry and thirsty,
they nearly died.

⁶ "LORD, help!" they cried in their trouble,
and he rescued them from their distress.
⁷ He led them straight to safety,
to a city where they could live.
⁸ Let them praise the LORD for his great love
and for the wonderful things he has
done for them.
⁹ For he satisfies the thirsty
and fills the hungry with good things.

¹⁰ Some sat in darkness and deepest gloom,
imprisoned in iron chains of misery.
¹¹ They rebelled against the words of God,
scorning the counsel of the Most High.
¹² That is why he broke them with hard
labor;
they fell, and no one was there to help
them.
¹³ "LORD, help!" they cried in their trouble,
and he saved them from their distress.
¹⁴ He led them from the darkness and
deepest gloom;
he snapped their chains.
¹⁵ Let them praise the LORD for his great love
and for the wonderful things he has
done for them.
¹⁶ For he broke down their prison gates of
bronze;
he cut apart their bars of iron.

¹⁷ Some were fools; they rebelled
and suffered for their sins.
¹⁸ They couldn't stand the thought of food,
and they were knocking on death's door.
¹⁹ "LORD, help!" they cried in their trouble,
and he saved them from their distress.
²⁰ He sent out his word and healed them,
snatching them from the door of death.
²¹ Let them praise the LORD for his great love
and for the wonderful things he has
done for them.
²² Let them offer sacrifices of thanksgiving
and sing joyfully about his glorious acts.

²³ Some went off to sea in ships,
plying the trade routes of the world.
²⁴ They, too, observed the LORD's power in
action,
his impressive works on the deepest
seas.
²⁵ He spoke, and the winds rose,
stirring up the waves.
²⁶ Their ships were tossed to the heavens
and plunged again to the depths;
the sailors cringed in terror.

106:7 Hebrew *at the sea, the sea of reeds.* **106:9** Hebrew *sea of reeds;*
also in 106:22. **106:19** Hebrew *at Horeb,* another name for Sinai.
106:33 Hebrew *They embittered his spirit.*

²⁷ They reeled and staggered like drunkards
and were at their wits' end.
²⁸ "LORD, help!" they cried in their trouble,
and he saved them from their distress.
²⁹ He calmed the storm to a whisper
and stilled the waves.
³⁰ What a blessing was that stillness
as he brought them safely into harbor!
³¹ Let them praise the LORD for his great love
and for the wonderful things he has
done for them.
³² Let them exalt him publicly before the
congregation
and before the leaders of the nation.

³³ He changes rivers into deserts,
and springs of water into dry, thirsty
land.
³⁴ He turns the fruitful land into salty
wastelands,
because of the wickedness of those who
live there.
³⁵ But he also turns deserts into pools of
water,
the dry land into springs of water.
³⁶ He brings the hungry to settle there
and to build their cities.
³⁷ They sow their fields, plant their
vineyards,
and harvest their bumper crops.
³⁸ How he blesses them!
They raise large families there,
and their herds of livestock increase.

³⁹ When they decrease in number and
become impoverished
through oppression, trouble, and
sorrow,
⁴⁰ the LORD pours contempt on their princes,
causing them to wander in trackless
wastelands.
⁴¹ But he rescues the poor from trouble
and increases their families like flocks
of sheep.
⁴² The godly will see these things and be glad,
while the wicked are struck silent.
⁴³ Those who are wise will take all this to
heart;
they will see in our history the faithful
love of the LORD.

108 *A song. A psalm of David.*

¹ My heart is confident in you, O God;
no wonder I can sing your praises with
all my heart!

² Wake up, lyre and harp!
I will wake the dawn with my song.
³ I will thank you, LORD, among all the
people.
I will sing your praises among the
nations.
⁴ For your unfailing love is higher than the
heavens.
Your faithfulness reaches to the clouds.
⁵ Be exalted, O God, above the highest
heavens.
May your glory shine over all the earth.

⁶ Now rescue your beloved people.
Answer and save us by your power.
⁷ God has promised this by his holiness*:
"I will divide up Shechem with joy.
I will measure out the valley of Succoth.
⁸ Gilead is mine,
and Manasseh, too.
Ephraim, my helmet, will produce my
warriors,
and Judah, my scepter, will produce my
kings.
⁹ But Moab, my washbasin, will become my
servant,
and I will wipe my feet on Edom
and shout in triumph over Philistia."

¹⁰ Who will bring me into the fortified city?
Who will bring me victory over Edom?
¹¹ Have you rejected us, O God?
Will you no longer march with our
armies?
¹² Oh, please help us against our enemies,
for all human help is useless.
¹³ With God's help we will do mighty
things,
for he will trample down our foes.

109 *For the choir director: A psalm of David.*

¹ O God, whom I praise,
don't stand silent and aloof
² while the wicked slander me
and tell lies about me.
³ They surround me with hateful words
and fight against me for no reason.
⁴ I love them, but they try to destroy me
with accusations
even as I am praying for them!
⁵ They repay evil for good,
and hatred for my love.

⁶ They say,* "Get an evil person to turn
against him.
Send an accuser to bring him to trial.

⁷ When his case comes up for judgment,
    let him be pronounced guilty.
    Count his prayers as sins.
⁸ Let his years be few;
    let someone else take his position.
⁹ May his children become fatherless,
    and his wife a widow.
¹⁰ May his children wander as beggars
    and be driven from their ruined homes.
¹¹ May creditors seize his entire estate,
    and strangers take all he has earned.
¹² Let no one be kind to him;
    let no one pity his fatherless children.
¹³ May all his offspring die.
    May his family name be blotted out in a
    single generation.
¹⁴ May the LORD never forget the sins of his
    fathers;
    may his mother's sins never be erased
    from the record.
¹⁵ May the LORD always remember these
    sins,
    and may his name disappear from
    human memory.
¹⁶ For he refused all kindness to others;
    he persecuted the poor and needy,
    and he hounded the brokenhearted to
    death.
¹⁷ He loved to curse others;
    now you curse him.
    He never blessed others;
    now don't you bless him.
¹⁸ Cursing is as natural to him as his
    clothing,
    or the water he drinks,
    or the rich food he eats.
¹⁹ Now may his curses return and cling to
    him like clothing;
    may they be tied around him like a belt."

²⁰ May those curses become the LORD's
    punishment
    for my accusers who speak evil of me.
²¹ But deal well with me, O Sovereign LORD,
    for the sake of your own reputation!
    Rescue me
    because you are so faithful and good.
²² For I am poor and needy,
    and my heart is full of pain.
²³ I am fading like a shadow at dusk;
    I am brushed off like a locust.
²⁴ My knees are weak from fasting,
    and I am skin and bones.
²⁵ I am a joke to people everywhere;
    when they see me, they shake their
    heads in scorn.

²⁶ Help me, O LORD my God!
    Save me because of your unfailing love.
²⁷ Let them see that this is your doing,
    that you yourself have done it, LORD.
²⁸ Then let them curse me if they like,
    but you will bless me!
    When they attack me, they will be
    disgraced!
    But I, your servant, will go right on
    rejoicing!
²⁹ May my accusers be clothed with
    disgrace;
    may their humiliation cover them like a
    cloak.
³⁰ But I will give repeated thanks to the
    LORD,
    praising him to everyone.
³¹ For he stands beside the needy,
    ready to save them from those who
    condemn them.

110 *A psalm of David.*

¹ The LORD said to my Lord,
    "Sit in the place of honor at my right
    hand
    until I humble your enemies,
    making them a footstool under your
    feet."

² The LORD will extend your powerful
    kingdom from Jerusalem*;
    you will rule over your enemies.
³ When you go to war,
    your people will serve you willingly.
    You are arrayed in holy garments,
    and your strength will be renewed each
    day like the morning dew.

⁴ The LORD has taken an oath and will not
    break his vow:
    "You are a priest forever in the order of
    Melchizedek."

⁵ The Lord stands at your right hand to
    protect you.
    He will strike down many kings when
    his anger erupts.
⁶ He will punish the nations
    and fill their lands with corpses;
    he will shatter heads over the whole
    earth.
⁷ But he himself will be refreshed from
    brooks along the way.
    He will be victorious.

108:7 Or *in his sanctuary.*   **109:6** Hebrew lacks *They say.*
110:2 Hebrew *Zion.*

111

*¹ Praise the LORD!

I will thank the LORD with all my heart
as I meet with his godly people.
² How amazing are the deeds of the LORD!
All who delight in him should ponder them.
³ Everything he does reveals his glory and majesty.
His righteousness never fails.
⁴ He causes us to remember his wonderful works.
How gracious and merciful is our LORD!
⁵ He gives food to those who fear him;
he always remembers his covenant.
⁶ He has shown his great power to his people
by giving them the lands of other nations.
⁷ All he does is just and good,
and all his commandments are trustworthy.
⁸ They are forever true,
to be obeyed faithfully and with integrity.
⁹ He has paid a full ransom for his people.
He has guaranteed his covenant with them forever.
What a holy, awe-inspiring name he has!
¹⁰ Fear of the LORD is the foundation of true wisdom.
All who obey his commandments will grow in wisdom.

Praise him forever!

112

*¹ Praise the LORD!

How joyful are those who fear the LORD
and delight in obeying his commands.
² Their children will be successful everywhere;
an entire generation of godly people will be blessed.
³ They themselves will be wealthy,
and their good deeds will last forever.
⁴ Light shines in the darkness for the godly.
They are generous, compassionate, and righteous.
⁵ Good comes to those who lend money generously
and conduct their business fairly.
⁶ Such people will not be overcome by evil.
Those who are righteous will be long remembered.

⁷ They do not fear bad news;
they confidently trust the LORD to care for them.
⁸ They are confident and fearless
and can face their foes triumphantly.
⁹ They share freely and give generously to those in need.
Their good deeds will be remembered forever.
They will have influence and honor.
¹⁰ The wicked will see this and be infuriated.
They will grind their teeth in anger;
they will slink away, their hopes thwarted.

113

¹ Praise the LORD!

Yes, give praise, O servants of the LORD.
Praise the name of the LORD!
² Blessed be the name of the LORD
now and forever.
³ Everywhere—from east to west—
praise the name of the LORD.
⁴ For the LORD is high above the nations;
his glory is higher than the heavens.

⁵ Who can be compared with the LORD our God,
who is enthroned on high?
⁶ He stoops to look down
on heaven and on earth.
⁷ He lifts the poor from the dust
and the needy from the garbage dump.
⁸ He sets them among princes,
even the princes of his own people!
⁹ He gives the childless woman a family,
making her a happy mother.

Praise the LORD!

114

¹ When the Israelites escaped from Egypt—
when the family of Jacob left that foreign land—
² the land of Judah became God's sanctuary,
and Israel became his kingdom.

³ The Red Sea* saw them coming and hurried out of their way!
The water of the Jordan River turned away.
⁴ The mountains skipped like rams,
the hills like lambs!
⁵ What's wrong, Red Sea, that made you hurry out of their way?
What happened, Jordan River, that you turned away?

Long Remembered

OUR DAILY BREAD PSALM 112

A good deal of our unhappiness as we grow older is caused by our pining for the "good old days"—those times when we enjoyed health, wealth, position, or power. But the things of this world don't last. They are vacillating, changeable, capricious. In time, they may be taken away from us and replaced with poverty, isolation, weakness, and pain.

When we realize that this world and everything in it is unstable and unpredictable, we are left longing for something that lasts. What is left?

The psalmist wrote, "Those who are righteous will be long remembered" (112:6). Their righteousness is untouched and unharmed by time and circumstances. Nothing that happens in this world can take it away. It endures when life has stripped us of every other possession.

Righteousness is ours as we draw near to God through faith in Jesus Christ (see Rom 1:17; 3:21–26). He is our rock and our salvation and the only source of true and lasting happiness. Psalm 112:1 says, "How joyful are those who fear the LORD and delight in obeying his commands."

Delight in the Lord and in His Word, and you'll find true happiness. He alone offers a righteousness that endures for all eternity. —DHR

> **Those who are righteous will be long remembered. ...Their good deeds will be remembered forever.**
>
> PSALM 112:6–9

Lord, you are the only one who can bring satisfaction to our heart's longing for something that lasts. You alone bring joy for today and bright hope for tomorrow.

Happiness is ours when we delight in the Lord.

DAY 18: pg 75

---

⁶ Why, mountains, did you skip like rams?
    Why, hills, like lambs?
⁷ Tremble, O earth, at the presence of the Lord,
    at the presence of the God of Jacob.
⁸ He turned the rock into a pool of water;
    yes, a spring of water flowed from solid rock.

115 ¹ Not to us, O LORD, not to us,
    but to your name goes all the glory
for your unfailing love and faithfulness.
² Why let the nations say,
    "Where is their God?"

³ Our God is in the heavens,
    and he does as he wishes.
⁴ Their idols are merely things of silver and gold,
    shaped by human hands.
⁵ They have mouths but cannot speak,
    and eyes but cannot see.
⁶ They have ears but cannot hear,
    and noses but cannot smell.
⁷ They have hands but cannot feel,
    and feet but cannot walk,
    and throats but cannot make a sound.

111 This psalm is a Hebrew acrostic poem; after the introductory note of praise, each line begins with a successive letter of the Hebrew alphabet. 112 This psalm is a Hebrew acrostic poem; after the introductory note of praise, each line begins with a successive letter of the Hebrew alphabet. 114:3 Hebrew *the sea;* also in 114:5.

8 And those who make idols are just like
them,
as are all who trust in them.

9 O Israel, trust the LORD!
He is your helper and your shield.
10 O priests, descendants of Aaron, trust the
LORD!
He is your helper and your shield.
11 All you who fear the LORD, trust the LORD!
He is your helper and your shield.

12 The LORD remembers us and will bless us.
He will bless the people of Israel
and bless the priests, the descendants
of Aaron.
13 He will bless those who fear the LORD,
both great and lowly.

14 May the LORD richly bless
both you and your children.
15 May you be blessed by the LORD,
who made heaven and earth.
16 The heavens belong to the LORD,
but he has given the earth to all
humanity.
17 The dead cannot sing praises to the LORD,
for they have gone into the silence of the
grave.
18 But we can praise the LORD
both now and forever!

Praise the LORD!

116 1 I love the LORD because he hears
my voice
and my prayer for mercy.
2 Because he bends down to listen,
I will pray as long as I have breath!
3 Death wrapped its ropes around me;
the terrors of the grave* overtook me.
I saw only trouble and sorrow.
4 Then I called on the name of the LORD:
"Please, LORD, save me!"
5 How kind the LORD is! How good he is!
So merciful, this God of ours!
6 The LORD protects those of childlike
faith;
I was facing death, and he saved me.
7 Let my soul be at rest again,
for the LORD has been good to me.
8 He has saved me from death,
my eyes from tears,
my feet from stumbling.
9 And so I walk in the LORD's presence
as I live here on earth!
10 I believed in you, so I said,
"I am deeply troubled, LORD."

11 In my anxiety I cried out to you,
"These people are all liars!"
12 What can I offer the LORD
for all he has done for me?
13 I will lift up the cup of salvation
and praise the LORD's name for saving me.
14 I will keep my promises to the LORD
in the presence of all his people.

15 The LORD cares deeply
when his loved ones die.
16 O LORD, I am your servant;
yes, I am your servant, born into your
household;
you have freed me from my chains.
17 I will offer you a sacrifice of thanksgiving
and call on the name of the LORD.
18 I will fulfill my vows to the LORD
in the presence of all his people—
19 in the house of the LORD
in the heart of Jerusalem.

Praise the LORD!

117 1 Praise the LORD, all you nations.
Praise him, all you people of the
earth.
2 For he loves us with unfailing love;
the LORD's faithfulness endures forever.

Praise the LORD!

118 1 Give thanks to the LORD, for he is
good!
His faithful love endures forever.

2 Let all Israel repeat:
"His faithful love endures forever."
3 Let Aaron's descendants, the priests,
repeat:
"His faithful love endures forever."
4 Let all who fear the LORD repeat:
"His faithful love endures forever."

5 In my distress I prayed to the LORD,
and the LORD answered me and set me
free.
6 The LORD is for me, so I will have no fear.
What can mere people do to me?
7 Yes, the LORD is for me; he will help me.
I will look in triumph at those who
hate me.
8 It is better to take refuge in the LORD
than to trust in people.
9 It is better to take refuge in the LORD
than to trust in princes.

10 Though hostile nations surrounded me,
I destroyed them all with the authority
of the LORD.

The Awesome Power of God

OUR DAILY BREAD PSALM 114

B ack and forth, back and forth go the pounding waves of the sea. From ages past, the continents have been separated by the mighty oceans. Man has learned to travel over them, to descend to the bottom of them, and to travel through them—but their immensity and the relentless force of their waves remain untamable. Rocks are crushed, shorelines are changed, and even experienced sailors can be driven aground or sent to the bottom of the sea. The combined genius of man and the most powerful equipment can do little to conquer the oceans.

> Tremble, O earth, at the presence of the Lord.
>
> PSALM 114:7

They are no problem for God, however. The One who created the mighty oceans does with them what He wishes. Psalm 114 refers to the exodus of the Israelites from Egypt and the parting of the Red Sea (Exod 14:13–31) to describe God's great power. The psalmist wrote, "The Red Sea saw them coming and hurried out of their way!" (Ps 114:3). Then he asked, "What's wrong, Red Sea, that made you hurry out of their way?" (v. 5). The answer is implied: The seas were obeying the command of God.

When the turbulent seas of adversity are threatening, we need to remember the awesome power of God. As the seas fled before Him, so too can the obstacles that seem so overwhelming to us. They have no more resistance to God's power than water in a teacup! —DCE

What a mighty God we serve! I sing these words, Father, but many times I don't really understand or even contemplate your amazing, infinite power. Please help me to humbly bow before you, Most High God, knowing you can take care of whatever troubles I may face. Thank you, Father.

The power of God within you is greater than the pressure of troubles around you.

DAY 19: pg 77

11 Yes, they surrounded and attacked me,
    but I destroyed them all with the
      authority of the Lord.
12 They swarmed around me like
      bees;
    they blazed against me like a crackling
      fire.
    But I destroyed them all with the
      authority of the Lord.
13 My enemies did their best to kill me,
    but the Lord rescued me.

14 The Lord is my strength and my song;
    he has given me victory.
15 Songs of joy and victory are sung in the
      camp of the godly.
    The strong right arm of the Lord has
      done glorious things!
16 The strong right arm of the Lord is raised
      in triumph.
    The strong right arm of the Lord has
      done glorious things!

116:3 Hebrew *of Sheol.*

17 I will not die; instead, I will live
  to tell what the LORD has done.
18 The LORD has punished me severely,
  but he did not let me die.

19 Open for me the gates where the righteous
    enter,
  and I will go in and thank the LORD.
20 These gates lead to the presence of the
    LORD,
  and the godly enter there.
21 I thank you for answering my prayer
  and giving me victory!

22 The stone that the builders rejected
  has now become the cornerstone.
23 This is the LORD's doing,
  and it is wonderful to see.
24 This is the day the LORD has made.
  We will rejoice and be glad in it.
25 Please, LORD, please save us.
  Please, LORD, please give us success.
26 Bless the one who comes in the name of
    the LORD.
  We bless you from the house of the LORD.
27 The LORD is God, shining upon us.
  Take the sacrifice and bind it with cords
    on the altar.
28 You are my God, and I will praise you!
  You are my God, and I will exalt you!

29 Give thanks to the LORD, for he is good!
  His faithful love endures forever.

Aleph

119* ¹ Joyful are people of integrity,
    who follow the instructions of
      the LORD.
² Joyful are those who obey his laws
  and search for him with all their hearts.
³ They do not compromise with evil,
  and they walk only in his paths.
⁴ You have charged us
  to keep your commandments carefully.
⁵ Oh, that my actions would consistently
  reflect your decrees!
⁶ Then I will not be ashamed
  when I compare my life with your
    commands.
⁷ As I learn your righteous regulations,
  I will thank you by living as I should!
⁸ I will obey your decrees.
  Please don't give up on me!

Beth

⁹ How can a young person stay pure?
  By obeying your word.

¹⁰ I have tried hard to find you—
  don't let me wander from your commands.
¹¹ I have hidden your word in my heart,
  that I might not sin against you.
¹² I praise you, O LORD;
  teach me your decrees.
¹³ I have recited aloud
  all the regulations you have given us.
¹⁴ I have rejoiced in your laws
  as much as in riches.
¹⁵ I will study your commandments
  and reflect on your ways.
¹⁶ I will delight in your decrees
  and not forget your word.

Gimel

¹⁷ Be good to your servant,
  that I may live and obey your word.
¹⁸ Open my eyes to see
  the wonderful truths in your
    instructions.
¹⁹ I am only a foreigner in the land.
  Don't hide your commands from me!
²⁰ I am always overwhelmed
  with a desire for your regulations.
²¹ You rebuke the arrogant;
  those who wander from your commands
    are cursed.
²² Don't let them scorn and insult me,
  for I have obeyed your laws.
²³ Even princes sit and speak against me,
  but I will meditate on your decrees.
²⁴ Your laws please me;
  they give me wise advice.

Daleth

²⁵ I lie in the dust;
  revive me by your word.
²⁶ I told you my plans, and you answered.
  Now teach me your decrees.
²⁷ Help me understand the meaning of your
    commandments,
  and I will meditate on your wonderful
    deeds.
²⁸ I weep with sorrow;
  encourage me by your word.
²⁹ Keep me from lying to myself;
  give me the privilege of knowing your
    instructions.
³⁰ I have chosen to be faithful;
  I have determined to live by your
    regulations.
³¹ I cling to your laws.
  LORD, don't let me be put to shame!
³² I will pursue your commands,
  for you expand my understanding.

Untended Places

OUR DAILY BREAD PSALM 119:9–16

O ur family had just arrived at the lake cottage we had rented for a week of much-anticipated vacation when my wife discovered the unmistakable evidence of spiders and mice in the house. It wasn't that we had never encountered such things, but that we had expected the cottage to be cleaned and prepared for our stay there. Instead, the counters, cabinets, and beds were littered with the residue of infestation, requiring much cleaning before we settled in. It wasn't a bad house; it had just been left untended.

> I have hidden your word in my heart, that I might not sin against you.
>
> PSALM 119:11

We might be guilty of dealing with our hearts the way that cottage was managed. Our "untended places" can become breeding grounds for infestations of wrong thinking, poor attitudes, or sinful behavior—creating problems that require significant attention to correct. The wise path is to recognize our need to tend our hearts by staying in God's Word and embracing its truths.

In Psalm 119:11, the psalmist recognized the danger of not building our lives on the Scriptures. He said, "I have hidden your word in my heart, that I might not sin against you."

With a focus on the Word, we can build strong spiritual lives that will help us avoid the dangers that inevitably grow in untended places. —WEC

God, may your Word be our source for daily strength, encouragement, comfort when we're in pain, hope when we're facing despair, guidance when we've lost our way, and everlasting love that only comes from you.

To grow spiritually strong, read the Word.

DAY 20: pg 81

He

33 Teach me your decrees, O LORD;
  I will keep them to the end.
34 Give me understanding and I will obey
    your instructions;
  I will put them into practice with all my
  heart.
35 Make me walk along the path of your
    commands,
  for that is where my happiness is
  found.
36 Give me an eagerness for your laws
  rather than a love for money!
37 Turn my eyes from worthless things,
  and give me life through your word.*

38 Reassure me of your promise,
  made to those who fear you.
39 Help me abandon my shameful ways;
  for your regulations are good.
40 I long to obey your commandments!
  Renew my life with your goodness.

Waw

41 LORD, give me your unfailing love,
  the salvation that you promised me.
42 Then I can answer those who taunt me,
  for I trust in your word.

119 This psalm is a Hebrew acrostic poem; there are twenty-two stanzas, one for each successive letter of the Hebrew alphabet. Each of the eight verses within each stanza begins with the Hebrew letter named in its heading. **119:37** Some manuscripts read *in your ways.*

⁴³ Do not snatch your word of truth
from me,
for your regulations are my only hope.
⁴⁴ I will keep on obeying your instructions
forever and ever.
⁴⁵ I will walk in freedom,
for I have devoted myself to your
commandments.
⁴⁶ I will speak to kings about your laws,
and I will not be ashamed.
⁴⁷ How I delight in your commands!
How I love them!
⁴⁸ I honor and love your commands.
I meditate on your decrees.

Zayin

⁴⁹ Remember your promise to me;
it is my only hope.
⁵⁰ Your promise revives me;
it comforts me in all my troubles.
⁵¹ The proud hold me in utter contempt,
but I do not turn away from your
instructions.
⁵² I meditate on your age-old regulations;
O LORD, they comfort me.
⁵³ I become furious with the wicked,
because they reject your instructions.
⁵⁴ Your decrees have been the theme of my
songs
wherever I have lived.
⁵⁵ I reflect at night on who you are,
O LORD;
therefore, I obey your instructions.
⁵⁶ This is how I spend my life:
obeying your commandments.

Heth

⁵⁷ LORD, you are mine!
I promise to obey your words!
⁵⁸ With all my heart I want your blessings.
Be merciful as you promised.
⁵⁹ I pondered the direction of my life,
and I turned to follow your laws.
⁶⁰ I will hurry, without delay,
to obey your commands.
⁶¹ Evil people try to drag me into sin,
but I am firmly anchored to your
instructions.
⁶² I rise at midnight to thank you
for your just regulations.
⁶³ I am a friend to anyone who fears you—
anyone who obeys your
commandments.
⁶⁴ O LORD, your unfailing love fills the
earth;
teach me your decrees.

Teth

⁶⁵ You have done many good things for me,
LORD,
just as you promised.
⁶⁶ I believe in your commands;
now teach me good judgment and
knowledge.
⁶⁷ I used to wander off until you
disciplined me;
but now I closely follow your word.
⁶⁸ You are good and do only good;
teach me your decrees.
⁶⁹ Arrogant people smear me with lies,
but in truth I obey your commandments
with all my heart.
⁷⁰ Their hearts are dull and stupid,
but I delight in your instructions.
⁷¹ My suffering was good for me,
for it taught me to pay attention to your
decrees.
⁷² Your instructions are more valuable to me
than millions in gold and silver.

Yodh

⁷³ You made me; you created me.
Now give me the sense to follow your
commands.
⁷⁴ May all who fear you find in me a cause for
joy,
for I have put my hope in your word.
⁷⁵ I know, O LORD, that your regulations are
fair;
you disciplined me because I needed it.
⁷⁶ Now let your unfailing love comfort me,
just as you promised me, your servant.
⁷⁷ Surround me with your tender mercies so I
may live,
for your instructions are my delight.
⁷⁸ Bring disgrace upon the arrogant people
who lied about me;
meanwhile, I will concentrate on your
commandments.
⁷⁹ Let me be united with all who fear you,
with those who know your laws.
⁸⁰ May I be blameless in keeping your decrees;
then I will never be ashamed.

Kaph

⁸¹ I am worn out waiting for your rescue,
but I have put my hope in your word.
⁸² My eyes are straining to see your promises
come true.
When will you comfort me?
⁸³ I am shriveled like a wineskin in the smoke,
but I have not forgotten to obey your
decrees.

84 How long must I wait?
  When will you punish those who
    persecute me?
85 These arrogant people who hate your
    instructions
  have dug deep pits to trap me.
86 All your commands are trustworthy.
  Protect me from those who hunt me
    down without cause.
87 They almost finished me off,
  but I refused to abandon your
    commandments.
88 In your unfailing love, spare my life;
  then I can continue to obey your laws.

Lamedh

89 Your eternal word, O LORD,
  stands firm in heaven.
90 Your faithfulness extends to every
    generation,
  as enduring as the earth you created.
91 Your regulations remain true to this day,
  for everything serves your plans.
92 If your instructions hadn't sustained me
    with joy,
  I would have died in my misery.
93 I will never forget your commandments,
  for by them you give me life.
94 I am yours; rescue me!
  For I have worked hard at obeying your
    commandments.
95 Though the wicked hide along the way to
    kill me,
  I will quietly keep my mind on your laws.
96 Even perfection has its limits,
  but your commands have no limit.

Mem

97 Oh, how I love your instructions!
  I think about them all day long.
98 Your commands make me wiser than my
    enemies,
  for they are my constant guide.
99 Yes, I have more insight than my
    teachers,
  for I am always thinking of your laws.
100 I am even wiser than my elders,
  for I have kept your commandments.
101 I have refused to walk on any evil path,
  so that I may remain obedient to your
    word.
102 I haven't turned away from your
    regulations,
  for you have taught me well.
103 How sweet your words taste to me;
  they are sweeter than honey.

104 Your commandments give me
    understanding;
  no wonder I hate every false way of life.

Nun

105 Your word is a lamp to guide my feet
  and a light for my path.
106 I've promised it once, and I'll promise it
    again:
  I will obey your righteous regulations.
107 I have suffered much, O LORD;
  restore my life again as you promised.
108 LORD, accept my offering of praise,
  and teach me your regulations.
109 My life constantly hangs in the balance,
  but I will not stop obeying your
    instructions.
110 The wicked have set their traps for me,
  but I will not turn from your
    commandments.
111 Your laws are my treasure;
  they are my heart's delight.
112 I am determined to keep your decrees
  to the very end.

Samekh

113 I hate those with divided loyalties,
  but I love your instructions.
114 You are my refuge and my shield;
  your word is my source of hope.
115 Get out of my life, you evil-minded people,
  for I intend to obey the commands of my
    God.
116 LORD, sustain me as you promised, that I
    may live!
  Do not let my hope be crushed.
117 Sustain me, and I will be rescued;
  then I will meditate continually on your
    decrees.
118 But you have rejected all who stray from
    your decrees.
  They are only fooling themselves.
119 You skim off the wicked of the earth like
    scum;
  no wonder I love to obey your laws!
120 I tremble in fear of you;
  I stand in awe of your regulations.

Ayin

121 Don't leave me to the mercy of my
    enemies,
  for I have done what is just and right.
122 Please guarantee a blessing for me.
  Don't let the arrogant oppress me!
123 My eyes strain to see your rescue,
  to see the truth of your promise fulfilled.

¹²⁴ I am your servant; deal with me in
    unfailing love,
  and teach me your decrees.
¹²⁵ Give discernment to me, your servant;
  then I will understand your laws.
¹²⁶ LORD, it is time for you to act,
  for these evil people have violated your
    instructions.
¹²⁷ Truly, I love your commands
  more than gold, even the finest gold.
¹²⁸ Each of your commandments is right.
  That is why I hate every false way.

Pe

¹²⁹ Your laws are wonderful.
  No wonder I obey them!
¹³⁰ The teaching of your word gives light,
  so even the simple can understand.
¹³¹ I pant with expectation,
  longing for your commands.
¹³² Come and show me your mercy,
  as you do for all who love your name.
¹³³ Guide my steps by your word,
  so I will not be overcome by evil.
¹³⁴ Ransom me from the oppression of evil
    people;
  then I can obey your commandments.
¹³⁵ Look upon me with love;
  teach me your decrees.
¹³⁶ Rivers of tears gush from my eyes
  because people disobey your
    instructions.

Tsadhe

¹³⁷ O LORD, you are righteous,
  and your regulations are fair.
¹³⁸ Your laws are perfect
  and completely trustworthy.
¹³⁹ I am overwhelmed with indignation,
  for my enemies have disregarded your
    words.
¹⁴⁰ Your promises have been thoroughly tested;
  that is why I love them so much.
¹⁴¹ I am insignificant and despised,
  but I don't forget your commandments.
¹⁴² Your justice is eternal,
  and your instructions are perfectly true.
¹⁴³ As pressure and stress bear down on me,
  I find joy in your commands.
¹⁴⁴ Your laws are always right;
  help me to understand them so I may
    live.

Qoph

¹⁴⁵ I pray with all my heart; answer me, LORD!
  I will obey your decrees.

¹⁴⁶ I cry out to you; rescue me,
  that I may obey your laws.
¹⁴⁷ I rise early, before the sun is up;
  I cry out for help and put my hope in
    your words.
¹⁴⁸ I stay awake through the night,
  thinking about your promise.
¹⁴⁹ In your faithful love, O LORD, hear my cry;
  let me be revived by following your
    regulations.
¹⁵⁰ Lawless people are coming to attack me;
  they live far from your instructions.
¹⁵¹ But you are near, O LORD,
  and all your commands are true.
¹⁵² I have known from my earliest days
  that your laws will last forever.

Resh

¹⁵³ Look upon my suffering and rescue me,
  for I have not forgotten your
    instructions.
¹⁵⁴ Argue my case; take my side!
  Protect my life as you promised.
¹⁵⁵ The wicked are far from rescue,
  for they do not bother with your decrees.
¹⁵⁶ LORD, how great is your mercy;
  let me be revived by following your
    regulations.
¹⁵⁷ Many persecute and trouble me,
  yet I have not swerved from your laws.
¹⁵⁸ Seeing these traitors makes me sick at
    heart,
  because they care nothing for your word.
¹⁵⁹ See how I love your commandments, LORD.
  Give back my life because of your
    unfailing love.
¹⁶⁰ The very essence of your words is truth;
  all your just regulations will stand forever.

Shin

¹⁶¹ Powerful people harass me without cause,
  but my heart trembles only at your word.
¹⁶² I rejoice in your word
  like one who discovers a great treasure.
¹⁶³ I hate and abhor all falsehood,
  but I love your instructions.
¹⁶⁴ I will praise you seven times a day
  because all your regulations are just.
¹⁶⁵ Those who love your instructions have
    great peace
  and do not stumble.
¹⁶⁶ I long for your rescue, LORD,
  so I have obeyed your commands.
¹⁶⁷ I have obeyed your laws,
  for I love them very much.
¹⁶⁸ Yes, I obey your commandments and laws
  because you know everything I do.

Meditate on These Things

OUR DAILY BREAD PSALM 119:105–136

Some Christians get a little skeptical when you start talking about meditation—not seeing the huge distinction between biblical meditation and some types of mystical meditation. In mystical meditation, according to one explanation, "the rational mind is shifted into neutral . . . so that the psyche can take over." The focus is inward, and the aim is to "become one with God."

> Sustain me, and I will be rescued; then I will meditate continually on your decrees.
>
> PSALM 119:117

In contrast, biblical meditation focuses on the things of the Lord, and its purpose is to renew our minds (Rom 12:2) so that we think and act more like Christ. Its objective is to reflect on what God has said and done (Ps 77:12; 119:15–16, 97) and on what He is like (48:9–14).

In Psalm 19:14, David wrote, "May the words of my mouth and the meditation of my heart be pleasing to you, O LORD, my rock and my redeemer." Other psalms reflect on God's love (48:9), His mighty works (77:12), His instructions (119:97), and His laws (119:99).

Fill your mind with Scripture and focus on the Lord's commands and promises and goodness. And remember this: Whatever is true, noble, just, pure, lovely, and of good report, meditate on these things (Phil 4:8). —CHK

Lord, lead me to meditate on your Word, so that I may know you better, become more like your Son, and please you in all I do and say.

- - - - - - - - - - - - - - - - - - - **To become more like Christ, meditate on who He is.** - - - - - - - - - - - - - - - - - - -

DAY 21: pg 83

Taw

169 O LORD, listen to my cry;
　　give me the discerning mind you promised.
170 Listen to my prayer;
　　rescue me as you promised.
171 Let praise flow from my lips,
　　for you have taught me your decrees.
172 Let my tongue sing about your word,
　　for all your commands are right.
173 Give me a helping hand,
　　for I have chosen to follow your
　　　　commandments.
174 O LORD, I have longed for your rescue,
　　and your instructions are my delight.
175 Let me live so I can praise you,
　　and may your regulations help me.
176 I have wandered away like a lost sheep;
　　come and find me,
　　for I have not forgotten your commands.

120

A song for pilgrims ascending to Jerusalem.

1 I took my troubles to the LORD;
　　I cried out to him, and he answered my
　　　　prayer.
2 Rescue me, O LORD, from liars
　　and from all deceitful people.
3 O deceptive tongue, what will God do to
　　　　you?
　　How will he increase your punishment?
4 You will be pierced with sharp arrows
　　and burned with glowing coals.

5 How I suffer in far-off Meshech.
　　It pains me to live in distant Kedar.
6 I am tired of living
　　among people who hate peace.
7 I search for peace;
　　but when I speak of peace, they want war!

121 A song for pilgrims ascending to Jerusalem.

1 I look up to the mountains—
   does my help come from there?
2 My help comes from the LORD,
   who made heaven and earth!

3 He will not let you stumble;
   the one who watches over you will not
   slumber.
4 Indeed, he who watches over Israel
   never slumbers or sleeps.

5 The LORD himself watches over you!
   The LORD stands beside you as your
   protective shade.
6 The sun will not harm you by day,
   nor the moon at night.

7 The LORD keeps you from all harm
   and watches over your life.
8 The LORD keeps watch over you as you
   come and go,
   both now and forever.

122 A song for pilgrims ascending to Jerusalem. A psalm of David.

1 I was glad when they said to me,
   "Let us go to the house of the LORD."
2 And now here we are,
   standing inside your gates,
   O Jerusalem.
3 Jerusalem is a well-built city;
   its seamless walls cannot be
   breached.
4 All the tribes of Israel—the LORD's
   people—
   make their pilgrimage here.
   They come to give thanks to the name of
   the LORD,
   as the law requires of Israel.
5 Here stand the thrones where judgment is
   given,
   the thrones of the dynasty of David.

6 Pray for peace in Jerusalem.
   May all who love this city prosper.
7 O Jerusalem, may there be peace within
   your walls
   and prosperity in your palaces.
8 For the sake of my family and friends,
   I will say,
   "May you have peace."
9 For the sake of the house of the LORD our
   God,
   I will seek what is best for you,
   O Jerusalem.

123 A song for pilgrims ascending to Jerusalem.

1 I lift my eyes to you,
   O God, enthroned in heaven.
2 We keep looking to the LORD our God for
   his mercy,
   just as servants keep their eyes on their
   master,
   as a slave girl watches her mistress for
   the slightest signal.
3 Have mercy on us, LORD, have mercy,
   for we have had our fill of contempt.
4 We have had more than our fill of the
   scoffing of the proud
   and the contempt of the arrogant.

124 A song for pilgrims ascending to Jerusalem. A psalm of David.

1 What if the LORD had not been on our side?
   Let all Israel repeat:
2 What if the LORD had not been on our side
   when people attacked us?
3 They would have swallowed us alive
   in their burning anger.
4 The waters would have engulfed us;
   a torrent would have overwhelmed us.
5 Yes, the raging waters of their fury
   would have overwhelmed our very lives.

6 Praise the LORD,
   who did not let their teeth tear us apart!
7 We escaped like a bird from a hunter's trap.
   The trap is broken, and we are free!
8 Our help is from the LORD,
   who made heaven and earth.

125 A song for pilgrims ascending to Jerusalem.

1 Those who trust in the LORD are as secure
   as Mount Zion;
   they will not be defeated but will endure
   forever.
2 Just as the mountains surround Jerusalem,
   so the LORD surrounds his people, both
   now and forever.
3 The wicked will not rule the land of the
   godly,
   for then the godly might be tempted to
   do wrong.
4 O LORD, do good to those who are good,
   whose hearts are in tune with you.
5 But banish those who turn to crooked
   ways, O LORD.
   Take them away with those who do evil.

May Israel have peace!

What's in Your Mouth?

Communications experts tell us that the average person speaks enough to fill 20 single-spaced, typed pages every day. This means our mouths crank out enough words to fill two books of 300 pages each month, 24 books each year, and 1,200 books in 50 years of speaking. Thanks to phones, voicemail, and face-to-face conversations, words comprise a large part of our lives. So the kinds of words we use are important.

> We were filled with laughter, and we sang for joy. And the other nations said, "What amazing things the LORD has done for them."
>
> PSALM 126:2

The psalmist's mouth was filled with praise when he wrote Psalm 126. The Lord had done great things for him and his people. Even the nations around them noticed. Remembering God's blessings, he said, "We were filled with laughter, and we sang for joy" (v. 2).

What words would you have used in verse 3 had you been writing this psalm? So often, our attitude may seem to be: "The LORD has done amazing things" for me, and I—

... can't recall any of them right now.

... am wondering what He'll do for me next.

... need much more.

Or can you finish it by saying, "And I am praising and thanking Him for His goodness"? As you recall God's blessings today, express your words of praise to Him. —AMC

Help me, O God, to use words that reflect you and your love today. Help me to speak kind and encouraging words to the people I know or work with. Help me to use compassionate words on those who need assistance. And help me to use words of love and nurturing for the people in my family.

Let no thought linger in your mind that you would be ashamed to let out of your mouth. DAY 22: pg 85

126 *A song for pilgrims ascending to Jerusalem.*

¹ When the LORD brought back his exiles to Jerusalem,*
it was like a dream!
² We were filled with laughter,
and we sang for joy.
And the other nations said,
"What amazing things the LORD has done for them."
³ Yes, the LORD has done amazing things for us!
What joy!

⁴ Restore our fortunes, LORD,
as streams renew the desert.
⁵ Those who plant in tears
will harvest with shouts of joy.
⁶ They weep as they go to plant their seed,
but they sing as they return with the harvest.

127 *A song for pilgrims ascending to Jerusalem. A psalm of Solomon.*

¹ Unless the LORD builds a house,
the work of the builders is wasted.

126:1 Hebrew *Zion.*

Unless the LORD protects a city,
    guarding it with sentries will do no
        good.
2 It is useless for you to work so hard
    from early morning until late at night,
    anxiously working for food to eat;
        for God gives rest to his loved ones.

3 Children are a gift from the LORD;
    they are a reward from him.
4 Children born to a young man
    are like arrows in a warrior's hands.
5 How joyful is the man whose quiver is full
        of them!
    He will not be put to shame when he
        confronts his accusers at the city gates.

128 *A song for pilgrims ascending
to Jerusalem.*

1 How joyful are those who fear the LORD—
    all who follow his ways!
2 You will enjoy the fruit of your labor.
    How joyful and prosperous you will be!
3 Your wife will be like a fruitful grapevine,
    flourishing within your home.
    Your children will be like vigorous young
        olive trees
    as they sit around your table.
4 That is the LORD's blessing
    for those who fear him.

5 May the LORD continually bless you from
        Zion.
    May you see Jerusalem prosper as long
        as you live.
6 May you live to enjoy your grandchildren.
    May Israel have peace!

129 *A song for pilgrims ascending
to Jerusalem.*

1 From my earliest youth my enemies have
        persecuted me.
    Let all Israel repeat this:
2 From my earliest youth my enemies have
        persecuted me,
    but they have never defeated me.
3 My back is covered with cuts,
    as if a farmer had plowed long furrows.
4 But the LORD is good;
    he has cut me free from the ropes of the
        ungodly.

5 May all who hate Jerusalem*
    be turned back in shameful defeat.
6 May they be as useless as grass on a rooftop,
    turning yellow when only half grown,

7 ignored by the harvester,
    despised by the binder.
8 And may those who pass by
    refuse to give them this blessing:
    "The LORD bless you;
        we bless you in the LORD's name."

130 *A song for pilgrims ascending
to Jerusalem.*

1 From the depths of despair, O LORD,
    I call for your help.
2 Hear my cry, O Lord.
    Pay attention to my prayer.

3 LORD, if you kept a record of our sins,
    who, O Lord, could ever survive?
4 But you offer forgiveness,
    that we might learn to fear you.

5 I am counting on the LORD;
    yes, I am counting on him.
    I have put my hope in his word.
6 I long for the Lord
    more than sentries long for the dawn,
    yes, more than sentries long for the
        dawn.

7 O Israel, hope in the LORD;
    for with the LORD there is unfailing love.
    His redemption overflows.
8 He himself will redeem Israel
    from every kind of sin.

131 *A song for pilgrims ascending
to Jerusalem. A psalm of David.*

1 LORD, my heart is not proud;
    my eyes are not haughty.
    I don't concern myself with matters too
        great
    or too awesome for me to grasp.
2 Instead, I have calmed and quieted
        myself,
    like a weaned child who no longer cries
        for its mother's milk.
    Yes, like a weaned child is my soul
        within me.

3 O Israel, put your hope in the LORD—
    now and always.

132 *A song for pilgrims ascending
to Jerusalem.*

1 LORD, remember David
    and all that he suffered.
2 He made a solemn promise to the LORD.
    He vowed to the Mighty One of Israel,*

Path to Humility

OUR DAILY BREAD PSALM 131

My friend declared, as he tried to keep a straight face, "I'm so proud of my humility!" That reminds me of the joke about a leader who was given an award for his humility. Because he accepted the award, it was taken back the following week!

David seemed to be making the same error when he said, "My heart is not proud" (Ps 131:1). When we understand the text, however, we know that he wasn't boasting about his humility. Rather, in response to the accusation of treason made by Saul's men, David stated he didn't consider himself so important nor think of himself so highly as to have "haughty" eyes.

> LORD, my heart is not proud; my eyes are not haughty.
>
> PSALM 131:1

Instead, David learned to be like a "weaned child" in the Lord's arms (v. 2). Like a baby who is completely dependent on his parents, he waited on God for His protection while he was a fugitive under King Saul's pursuit. In his darkest hour, David realized his need and then advised his people: "Put your hope in the LORD—now and always" (v. 3).

The path to humility is twofold. It involves knowing who we are—having a proper self-esteem rather than thinking too highly of self. But most important, it requires knowing who God is—holding Him in highest esteem and trusting Him for His best in His time. —AL

Lord, give me the humility I lack to admit my mistakes. Give me wisdom to know when I need the help and advice of others. Help me to be obedient and dependent on you to guide my way.

When we think we're humble—
we're not.

DAY 23: pg 88

³ "I will not go home;
  I will not let myself rest.
⁴ I will not let my eyes sleep
  nor close my eyelids in slumber
⁵ until I find a place to build a house for the LORD,
  a sanctuary for the Mighty One of Israel."

⁶ We heard that the Ark was in Ephrathah;
  then we found it in the distant countryside of Jaar.
⁷ Let us go to the sanctuary of the LORD;
  let us worship at the footstool of his throne.

⁸ Arise, O LORD, and enter your resting place,
  along with the Ark, the symbol of your power.
⁹ May your priests be clothed in godliness;
  may your loyal servants sing for joy.
¹⁰ For the sake of your servant David,
  do not reject the king you have anointed.
¹¹ The LORD swore an oath to David
  with a promise he will never take back:
  "I will place one of your descendants on your throne.

129:5 Hebrew *Zion*. 132:2 Hebrew *of Jacob*; also in 132:5. See note on 44:4.

¹² If your descendants obey the terms of my
      covenant
   and the laws that I teach them,
 then your royal line
   will continue forever and ever."

¹³ For the LORD has chosen Jerusalem*;
   he has desired it for his home.
¹⁴ "This is my resting place forever," he said.
   "I will live here, for this is the home I
      desired.
¹⁵ I will bless this city and make it
      prosperous;
   I will satisfy its poor with food.
¹⁶ I will clothe its priests with godliness;
   its faithful servants will sing for joy.
¹⁷ Here I will increase the power of David;
   my anointed one will be a light for my
      people.
¹⁸ I will clothe his enemies with shame,
   but he will be a glorious king."

133 *A song for pilgrims ascending
      to Jerusalem. A psalm of David.*

¹ How wonderful and pleasant it is
   when brothers live together in harmony!
² For harmony is as precious as the
      anointing oil
   that was poured over Aaron's head,
   that ran down his beard
   and onto the border of his robe.
³ Harmony is as refreshing as the dew from
      Mount Hermon
   that falls on the mountains of Zion.
 And there the LORD has pronounced his
      blessing,
   even life everlasting.

134 *A song for pilgrims ascending
      to Jerusalem.*

¹ Oh, praise the LORD, all you servants of
      the LORD,
   you who serve at night in the house of
      the LORD.
² Lift up holy hands in prayer,
   and praise the LORD.

³ May the LORD, who made heaven and
      earth,
   bless you from Jerusalem.*

135 ¹ Praise the LORD!

   Praise the name of the LORD!
 Praise him, you who serve the LORD,
² you who serve in the house of the LORD,
   in the courts of the house of our God.

³ Praise the LORD, for the LORD is good;
   celebrate his lovely name with music.
⁴ For the LORD has chosen Jacob for himself,
   Israel for his own special treasure.
⁵ I know the greatness of the LORD—
   that our Lord is greater than any other
      god.
⁶ The LORD does whatever pleases him
   throughout all heaven and earth,
   and on the seas and in their depths.
⁷ He causes the clouds to rise over the whole
      earth.
   He sends the lightning with the rain
   and releases the wind from his
      storehouses.
⁸ He destroyed the firstborn in each
      Egyptian home,
   both people and animals.
⁹ He performed miraculous signs and
      wonders in Egypt
   against Pharaoh and all his people.
¹⁰ He struck down great nations
   and slaughtered mighty kings—
¹¹ Sihon king of the Amorites,
   Og king of Bashan,
   and all the kings of Canaan.
¹² He gave their land as an inheritance,
   a special possession to his people Israel.

¹³ Your name, O LORD, endures forever;
   your fame, O LORD, is known to every
      generation.
¹⁴ For the LORD will give justice to his people
   and have compassion on his servants.

¹⁵ The idols of the nations are merely things
      of silver and gold,
   shaped by human hands.
¹⁶ They have mouths but cannot speak,
   and eyes but cannot see.
¹⁷ They have ears but cannot hear,
   and noses but cannot smell.
¹⁸ And those who make idols are just like
      them,
   as are all who trust in them.

¹⁹ O Israel, praise the LORD!
   O priests—descendants of Aaron—praise
      the LORD!
²⁰ O Levites, praise the LORD!
   All you who fear the LORD, praise the
      LORD!
²¹ The LORD be praised from Zion,
   for he lives here in Jerusalem.

 Praise the LORD!

136

¹ Give thanks to the LORD, for he is good!
His faithful love endures forever.
² Give thanks to the God of gods.
His faithful love endures forever.
³ Give thanks to the Lord of lords.
His faithful love endures forever.

⁴ Give thanks to him who alone does mighty miracles.
His faithful love endures forever.
⁵ Give thanks to him who made the heavens so skillfully.
His faithful love endures forever.
⁶ Give thanks to him who placed the earth among the waters.
His faithful love endures forever.
⁷ Give thanks to him who made the heavenly lights—
His faithful love endures forever.
⁸ the sun to rule the day,
His faithful love endures forever.
⁹ and the moon and stars to rule the night.
His faithful love endures forever.

¹⁰ Give thanks to him who killed the firstborn of Egypt.
His faithful love endures forever.
¹¹ He brought Israel out of Egypt.
His faithful love endures forever.
¹² He acted with a strong hand and powerful arm.
His faithful love endures forever.
¹³ Give thanks to him who parted the Red Sea.*
His faithful love endures forever.
¹⁴ He led Israel safely through,
His faithful love endures forever.
¹⁵ but he hurled Pharaoh and his army into the Red Sea.
His faithful love endures forever.
¹⁶ Give thanks to him who led his people through the wilderness.
His faithful love endures forever.

¹⁷ Give thanks to him who struck down mighty kings.
His faithful love endures forever.
¹⁸ He killed powerful kings—
His faithful love endures forever.
¹⁹ Sihon king of the Amorites,
His faithful love endures forever.
²⁰ and Og king of Bashan.
His faithful love endures forever.
²¹ God gave the land of these kings as an inheritance—
His faithful love endures forever.
²² a special possession to his servant Israel.
His faithful love endures forever.

²³ He remembered us in our weakness.
His faithful love endures forever.
²⁴ He saved us from our enemies.
His faithful love endures forever.
²⁵ He gives food to every living thing.
His faithful love endures forever.
²⁶ Give thanks to the God of heaven.
His faithful love endures forever.

137

¹ Beside the rivers of Babylon, we sat and wept
as we thought of Jerusalem.*
² We put away our harps,
hanging them on the branches of poplar trees.
³ For our captors demanded a song from us.
Our tormentors insisted on a joyful hymn:
"Sing us one of those songs of Jerusalem!"
⁴ But how can we sing the songs of the LORD
while in a pagan land?

⁵ If I forget you, O Jerusalem,
let my right hand forget how to play the harp.
⁶ May my tongue stick to the roof of my mouth
if I fail to remember you,
if I don't make Jerusalem my greatest joy.

⁷ O LORD, remember what the Edomites did
on the day the armies of Babylon
captured Jerusalem.
"Destroy it!" they yelled.
"Level it to the ground!"
⁸ O Babylon, you will be destroyed.
Happy is the one who pays you back
for what you have done to us.
⁹ Happy is the one who takes your babies
and smashes them against the rocks!

138

A psalm of David.

¹ I give you thanks, O LORD, with all my heart;
I will sing your praises before the gods.
² I bow before your holy Temple as I worship.
I praise your name for your unfailing love and faithfulness;
for your promises are backed
by all the honor of your name.
³ As soon as I pray, you answer me;
you encourage me by giving me strength.

⁴ Every king in all the earth will thank you, LORD,
for all of them will hear your words.
⁵ Yes, they will sing about the LORD's ways,
for the glory of the LORD is very great.

132:13 Hebrew *Zion*. **134:3** Hebrew *Zion*. **136:13** Hebrew *sea of reeds;* also in 136:15. **137:1** Hebrew *Zion;* also in 137:3.

DAY 23

What Color Is God?

OUR DAILY BREAD PSALM 139:1–12

What color is God? That's the question James McBride, an African-American author and musician, asked his Jewish mother when he was a boy. His autobiography contains the following story: Walking home from church one day, he asked her if God was black or white. She replied, "God is not black. God is not white. God is the color of water. Water doesn't have a color." That was indeed a wise response.

We know that God doesn't have a color because He doesn't have a body. He is Spirit and He's present everywhere (Ps 139:7–12). Whether we're sitting at home or flying miles above the earth, He is there and we can call out to Him. His ears are always open to our cry (Ps 34:15). He isn't an idol or a mere idea. God is Spirit, almighty, always present, ever available.

> I can never escape from your Spirit! I can never get away from your presence!
>
> PSALM 139:7

An atheist was engaged in a public debate with a Christian about the existence of God. To emphasize a point he was making, the atheist wrote these words on a blackboard: "God is nowhere." In rebuttal the Christian simply split the last word so that the statement read, "God is now here."

That truth can give us assurance, strength, and comfort each day as we trust in Him. —VCG

Thank you that you are almighty and always present with me. I know you hear my prayers because you are right here by my side. I am so thankful that I can never get away from your presence. I have your Spirit inside me, and one glorious day I will see you face-to-face!

Our greatest privilege is to enjoy God's presence.

DAY 24: pg 89

⁶ Though the LORD is great, he cares for the humble,
    but he keeps his distance from the proud.

⁷ Though I am surrounded by troubles,
    you will protect me from the anger of my enemies.
You reach out your hand,
    and the power of your right hand saves me.

⁸ The LORD will work out his plans for my life—
    for your faithful love, O LORD, endures forever.
Don't abandon me, for you made me.

139 *For the choir director: A psalm of David.*

¹ O LORD, you have examined my heart
    and know everything about me.
² You know when I sit down or stand up.
    You know my thoughts even when I'm far away.
³ You see me when I travel
    and when I rest at home.
    You know everything I do.
⁴ You know what I am going to say
    even before I say it, LORD.

Thinking of You

OUR DAILY BREAD PSALM 139:13–24

I was working alone in my office when a fax arrived from our daughter in Colorado. It had a goofy cartoon of a rabbit wearing a cowboy hat and chaps and swinging a lariat. "Well, howdy there, rancher Dave," it began, and ended with "I love you!"

It's a great feeling, isn't it, when a phone call or letter arrives from someone just to say, "I was thinking of you." It quickly banishes our sense of being alone.

The psalmist had a marvelous sense of God's personal care when he wrote: "How precious are your thoughts about me, O God. They cannot be numbered! I can't even count them; they outnumber the grains of sand! And when I wake up, you are still with me!" (Ps 139:17–18).

> How precious are your thoughts about me, O God. They cannot be numbered!
>
> PSALM 139:17

"When I wake up." We don't know David's circumstances when he wrote this psalm. He may have endured a night of fitful dozing, or he may have enjoyed a sound, peaceful sleep. Regardless, we know that David was overwhelmed by the knowledge that God was thinking of him even while he slept—so many thoughts he couldn't count them all.

The next time you feel alone, remember that God, who sent His Son to die for your sins, is thinking of you and saying, "I love you!" —DCM

Thank you, Father God, for loving me with a deep, unending love.
Thank you for sending your one and only Son to die in my place.
Thank you for thinking of me constantly day and night. Thank you
that I belong to you forever and ever. I love you, Abba Father.

Time spent alone with God can ease the pain of loneliness.

DAY 25: pg 91

⁵ You go before me and follow me.
   You place your hand of blessing on my head.
⁶ Such knowledge is too wonderful for me, too great for me to understand!

⁷ I can never escape from your Spirit!
   I can never get away from your presence!
⁸ If I go up to heaven, you are there;
   if I go down to the grave,* you are there.
⁹ If I ride the wings of the morning,
   if I dwell by the farthest oceans,
¹⁰ even there your hand will guide me,
   and your strength will support me.

¹¹ I could ask the darkness to hide me
   and the light around me to become night—
¹² but even in darkness I cannot hide from you.
To you the night shines as bright as day.
   Darkness and light are the same to you.

¹³ You made all the delicate, inner parts of my body
   and knit me together in my mother's womb.

139:8 Hebrew *to Sheol.*

¹⁴ Thank you for making me so wonderfully
complex!
Your workmanship is marvelous—how
well I know it.
¹⁵ You watched me as I was being formed in
utter seclusion,
as I was woven together in the dark of
the womb.
¹⁶ You saw me before I was born.
Every day of my life was recorded in
your book.
Every moment was laid out
before a single day had passed.

¹⁷ How precious are your thoughts about
me,* O God.
They cannot be numbered!
¹⁸ I can't even count them;
they outnumber the grains of sand!
And when I wake up,
you are still with me!

¹⁹ O God, if only you would destroy the wicked!
Get out of my life, you murderers!
²⁰ They blaspheme you;
your enemies misuse your name.
²¹ O LORD, shouldn't I hate those who hate
you?
Shouldn't I despise those who oppose
you?
²² Yes, I hate them with total hatred,
for your enemies are my enemies.

²³ Search me, O God, and know my heart;
test me and know my anxious thoughts.
²⁴ Point out anything in me that offends you,
and lead me along the path of
everlasting life.

140 *For the choir director:
A psalm of David.*

¹ O LORD, rescue me from evil people.
Protect me from those who are violent,
² those who plot evil in their hearts
and stir up trouble all day long.
³ Their tongues sting like a snake;
the venom of a viper drips from their
lips.   *Interlude*

⁴ O LORD, keep me out of the hands of the
wicked.
Protect me from those who are violent,
for they are plotting against me.
⁵ The proud have set a trap to catch me;
they have stretched out a net;
they have placed traps all along the way.
Interlude

⁶ I said to the LORD, "You are my God!"
Listen, O LORD, to my cries for mercy!
⁷ O Sovereign LORD, the strong one who
rescued me,
you protected me on the day of battle.
⁸ LORD, do not let evil people have their
way.
Do not let their evil schemes succeed,
or they will become proud.   *Interlude*

⁹ Let my enemies be destroyed
by the very evil they have planned for me.
¹⁰ Let burning coals fall down on their
heads.
Let them be thrown into the fire
or into watery pits from which they can't
escape.
¹¹ Don't let liars prosper here in our land.
Cause great disasters to fall on the
violent.

¹² But I know the LORD will help those they
persecute;
he will give justice to the poor.
¹³ Surely righteous people are praising your
name;
the godly will live in your presence.

141 *A psalm of David.*

¹ O LORD, I am calling to you. Please hurry!
Listen when I cry to you for help!
² Accept my prayer as incense offered to
you,
and my upraised hands as an evening
offering.

³ Take control of what I say, O LORD,
and guard my lips.
⁴ Don't let me drift toward evil
or take part in acts of wickedness.
Don't let me share in the delicacies
of those who do wrong.

⁵ Let the godly strike me!
It will be a kindness!
If they correct me, it is soothing medicine.
Don't let me refuse it.

But I pray constantly
against the wicked and their deeds.
⁶ When their leaders are thrown down from
a cliff,
the wicked will listen to my words and
find them true.
⁷ Like rocks brought up by a plow,
the bones of the wicked will lie scattered
without burial.*

Cracked Lenses

OUR DAILY BREAD PSALM 141

I started wearing glasses when I was ten years old. They are still a necessity because my fifty-something eyes are losing their battle against time. When I was younger, I thought glasses were a nuisance—especially when playing sports. Once, the lenses of my glasses got cracked while I was playing softball. It took several weeks to get them replaced. In the meantime, I saw everything in a skewed and distorted way.

In life, pain often functions like cracked lenses. It creates within us a conflict between what we experience and what we believe. Pain can give us a badly distorted perspective on life—and on God. In those times, we need our God to provide us with new lenses to help us see clearly again. That clarity of sight usually begins when we turn our eyes upon the Lord. The psalmist encouraged us to do this: "I look to you for help, O Sovereign LORD. You are my refuge; don't let them kill me" (Ps 141:8). Seeing God clearly can help us see life's experiences more clearly.

> I look to you for help, O Sovereign LORD.
>
> PSALM 141:8

As we turn our eyes to the Lord in times of pain and struggle, we will experience His comfort and hope in our daily lives. He will help us to see everything clearly again. —WEC

Lord, when my world is out of control, remind me to focus on you—to rest in your arms and to experience your never-ending grace.

Focusing on Christ puts everything in perspective.

DAY 26: pg 95

8 I look to you for help, O Sovereign LORD.
  You are my refuge; don't let them kill me.
9 Keep me from the traps they have set for me,
  from the snares of those who do wrong.
10 Let the wicked fall into their own nets,
  but let me escape.

142 *A psalm* of David, regarding his experience in the cave. A prayer.*

1 I cry out to the LORD;
  I plead for the LORD's mercy.
2 I pour out my complaints before him
  and tell him all my troubles.
3 When I am overwhelmed,
  you alone know the way I should turn.
  Wherever I go,
  my enemies have set traps for me.

4 I look for someone to come and help me,
  but no one gives me a passing
    thought!
No one will help me;
  no one cares a bit what happens to me.
5 Then I pray to you, O LORD.
  I say, "You are my place of refuge.
  You are all I really want in life.
6 Hear my cry,
  for I am very low.
Rescue me from my persecutors,
  for they are too strong for me.
7 Bring me out of prison
  so I can thank you.
The godly will crowd around me,
  for you are good to me."

139:17 Or *How precious to me are your thoughts.* **141:7** Hebrew *scattered at the mouth of Sheol.* **142:**TITLE Hebrew *maskil.* This may be a literary or musical term.

143 *A psalm of David.*

1 Hear my prayer, O LORD;
    listen to my plea!
    Answer me because you are faithful and
        righteous.
2 Don't put your servant on trial,
    for no one is innocent before you.
3 My enemy has chased me.
    He has knocked me to the ground
    and forces me to live in darkness like
        those in the grave.
4 I am losing all hope;
    I am paralyzed with fear.
5 I remember the days of old.
    I ponder all your great works
    and think about what you have done.
6 I lift my hands to you in prayer.
    I thirst for you as parched land thirsts
        for rain.   *Interlude*

7 Come quickly, LORD, and answer me,
    for my depression deepens.
    Don't turn away from me,
    or I will die.
8 Let me hear of your unfailing love each
        morning,
    for I am trusting you.
    Show me where to walk,
    for I give myself to you.
9 Rescue me from my enemies, LORD;
    I run to you to hide me.
10 Teach me to do your will,
    for you are my God.
    May your gracious Spirit lead me
        forward
    on a firm footing.
11 For the glory of your name, O LORD,
    preserve my life.
    Because of your faithfulness, bring me
        out of this distress.
12 In your unfailing love, silence all my
        enemies
    and destroy all my foes,
    for I am your servant.

144 *A psalm of David.*

1 Praise the LORD, who is my rock.
    He trains my hands for war
    and gives my fingers skill for battle.
2 He is my loving ally and my fortress,
    my tower of safety, my rescuer.
    He is my shield, and I take refuge in him.
    He makes the nations* submit to me.

3 O LORD, what are human beings that you
        should notice them,
    mere mortals that you should think
        about them?
4 For they are like a breath of air;
    their days are like a passing shadow.

5 Open the heavens, LORD, and come down.
    Touch the mountains so they billow
        smoke.
6 Hurl your lightning bolts and scatter your
        enemies!
    Shoot your arrows and confuse them!
7 Reach down from heaven and rescue me;
    rescue me from deep waters,
    from the power of my enemies.
8 Their mouths are full of lies;
    they swear to tell the truth, but they lie
        instead.

9 I will sing a new song to you, O God!
    I will sing your praises with a ten-
        stringed harp.
10 For you grant victory to kings!
    You rescued your servant David from the
        fatal sword.
11 Save me!
    Rescue me from the power of my enemies.
    Their mouths are full of lies;
    they swear to tell the truth, but they lie
        instead.

12 May our sons flourish in their youth
    like well-nurtured plants.
    May our daughters be like graceful pillars,
        carved to beautify a palace.
13 May our barns be filled
    with crops of every kind.
    May the flocks in our fields multiply by the
        thousands,
    even tens of thousands,
14   and may our oxen be loaded down with
        produce.
    May there be no enemy breaking through
        our walls,
    no going into captivity,
    no cries of alarm in our town squares.
15 Yes, joyful are those who live like this!
    Joyful indeed are those whose God is the
        LORD.

145 * *A psalm of praise of David.*

1 I will exalt you, my God and King,
    and praise your name forever and ever.
2 I will praise you every day;
    yes, I will praise you forever.

³ Great is the LORD! He is most worthy of
   praise!
   No one can measure his greatness.

⁴ Let each generation tell its children of
   your mighty acts;
   let them proclaim your power.
⁵ I will meditate* on your majestic, glorious
   splendor
   and your wonderful miracles.
⁶ Your awe-inspiring deeds will be on every
   tongue;
   I will proclaim your greatness.
⁷ Everyone will share the story of your
   wonderful goodness;
   they will sing with joy about your
   righteousness.

⁸ The LORD is merciful and compassionate,
   slow to get angry and filled with
   unfailing love.
⁹ The LORD is good to everyone.
   He showers compassion on all his
   creation.
¹⁰ All of your works will thank you, LORD,
   and your faithful followers will praise
   you.
¹¹ They will speak of the glory of your
   kingdom;
   they will give examples of your power.
¹² They will tell about your mighty deeds
   and about the majesty and glory of your
   reign.
¹³ For your kingdom is an everlasting
   kingdom.
   You rule throughout all generations.

The LORD always keeps his promises;
   he is gracious in all he does.*
¹⁴ The LORD helps the fallen
   and lifts those bent beneath their loads.
¹⁵ The eyes of all look to you in hope;
   you give them their food as they need it.
¹⁶ When you open your hand,
   you satisfy the hunger and thirst of
   every living thing.
¹⁷ The LORD is righteous in everything he
   does;
   he is filled with kindness.
¹⁸ The LORD is close to all who call on him,
   yes, to all who call on him in truth.
¹⁹ He grants the desires of those who fear
   him;
   he hears their cries for help and rescues
   them.
²⁰ The LORD protects all those who love him,
   but he destroys the wicked.

²¹ I will praise the LORD,
   and may everyone on earth bless his
   holy name
   forever and ever.

146 ¹ Praise the LORD!
   Let all that I am praise the LORD.
²   I will praise the LORD as long as I live.
   I will sing praises to my God with my
   dying breath.

³ Don't put your confidence in powerful
   people;
   there is no help for you there.
⁴ When they breathe their last, they return
   to the earth,
   and all their plans die with them.
⁵ But joyful are those who have the God of
   Israel* as their helper,
   whose hope is in the LORD their God.
⁶ He made heaven and earth,
   the sea, and everything in them.
   He keeps every promise forever.
⁷ He gives justice to the oppressed
   and food to the hungry.
   The LORD frees the prisoners.
⁸   The LORD opens the eyes of the blind.
   The LORD lifts up those who are weighed
   down.
   The LORD loves the godly.
⁹ The LORD protects the foreigners
   among us.
   He cares for the orphans and widows,
   but he frustrates the plans of the
   wicked.

¹⁰ The LORD will reign forever.
   He will be your God, O Jerusalem,*
   throughout the generations.

Praise the LORD!

147 ¹ Praise the LORD!
   How good to sing praises to our
   God!
   How delightful and how fitting!
² The LORD is rebuilding Jerusalem
   and bringing the exiles back to Israel.
³ He heals the brokenhearted
   and bandages their wounds.
⁴ He counts the stars
   and calls them all by name.

144:2 Some manuscripts read *my people*. **145** This psalm is a Hebrew
acrostic poem; each verse (including 13b) begins with a successive
letter of the Hebrew alphabet. **145:5** Some manuscripts read *They
will speak*. **145:13** The last two lines of 145:13 are not found in many
of the ancient manuscripts. **146:5** Hebrew *of Jacob*. See note on 44:4.
146:10 Hebrew *Zion*.

⁵ How great is our Lord! His power is
   absolute!
   His understanding is beyond
   comprehension!
⁶ The LORD supports the humble,
   but he brings the wicked down into the
   dust.

⁷ Sing out your thanks to the LORD;
   sing praises to our God with a harp.
⁸ He covers the heavens with clouds,
   provides rain for the earth,
   and makes the grass grow in mountain
   pastures.
⁹ He gives food to the wild animals
   and feeds the young ravens when they
   cry.
¹⁰ He takes no pleasure in the strength of a
   horse
   or in human might.
¹¹ No, the LORD's delight is in those who fear
   him,
   those who put their hope in his
   unfailing love.

¹² Glorify the LORD, O Jerusalem!
   Praise your God, O Zion!
¹³ For he has strengthened the bars of your
   gates
   and blessed your children within your
   walls.
¹⁴ He sends peace across your nation
   and satisfies your hunger with the finest
   wheat.
¹⁵ He sends his orders to the world—
   how swiftly his word flies!
¹⁶ He sends the snow like white wool;
   he scatters frost upon the ground like
   ashes.
¹⁷ He hurls the hail like stones.*
   Who can stand against his freezing
   cold?
¹⁸ Then, at his command, it all melts.
   He sends his winds, and the ice thaws.
¹⁹ He has revealed his words to Jacob,
   his decrees and regulations to Israel.
²⁰ He has not done this for any other
   nation;
   they do not know his regulations.

   Praise the LORD!

148

¹ Praise the LORD!
   Praise the LORD from the heavens!
   Praise him from the skies!
² Praise him, all his angels!
   Praise him, all the armies of heaven!

³ Praise him, sun and moon!
   Praise him, all you twinkling stars!
⁴ Praise him, skies above!
   Praise him, vapors high above the
   clouds!
⁵ Let every created thing give praise to the
   LORD,
   for he issued his command, and they
   came into being.
⁶ He set them in place forever and ever.
   His decree will never be revoked.

⁷ Praise the LORD from the earth,
   you creatures of the ocean depths,
⁸ fire and hail, snow and clouds,*
   wind and weather that obey him,
⁹ mountains and all hills,
   fruit trees and all cedars,
¹⁰ wild animals and all livestock,
   small scurrying animals and birds,
¹¹ kings of the earth and all people,
   rulers and judges of the earth,
¹² young men and young women,
   old men and children.

¹³ Let them all praise the name of the
   LORD.
   For his name is very great;
   his glory towers over the earth and
   heaven!
¹⁴ He has made his people strong,
   honoring his faithful ones—
   the people of Israel who are close to
   him.

   Praise the LORD!

149

¹ Praise the LORD!
   Sing to the LORD a new song.
   Sing his praises in the assembly of the
   faithful.

² O Israel, rejoice in your Maker.
   O people of Jerusalem,* exult in your
   King.
³ Praise his name with dancing,
   accompanied by tambourine and harp.
⁴ For the LORD delights in his people;
   he crowns the humble with victory.
⁵ Let the faithful rejoice that he honors
   them.
   Let them sing for joy as they lie on their
   beds.

⁶ Let the praises of God be in their mouths,
   and a sharp sword in their hands—
⁷ to execute vengeance on the nations
   and punishment on the peoples,

Psalms, Incense, Praise

OUR DAILY BREAD PSALM 150

The well-known English preacher Charles H. Spurgeon (1834–1892) wrote something that would be good to remember at the start of each day: "Let your thoughts be psalms, your prayers incense, and your breath praise." Let's look at each of these phrases.

Let your thoughts be psalms. The 150 psalms have a variety of themes, including praise, God's character, and expressions of dependence on the Lord. Throughout the day we can turn our thoughts into psalms by meditating on God's holiness, His worthiness of our worship, and how much we need Him.

Let your prayers be incense. In the tabernacle of the Jews, incense was burned continually to offer a sweet savor to the Lord (Exod 30:7–8). Our prayers are like incense to God (Ps 141:2), bringing to His nostrils the pleasing scent of our adoration and need for Him.

Let your breath be praise. The book of Psalms concludes with the words, "Let everything that breathes sing praises to the LORD! Praise the LORD!" (150:6). Talking about God and offering Him words of praise should be as natural to us as breathing.

Keep the Lord in your thoughts, prayers, and speech today. —DCE

> Let everything that breathes sing praises to the LORD! Praise the LORD!
>
> PSALM 150:6

Heavenly Father, you are great and worthy of praise. May our thoughts, prayers, and words bring you the highest glory you so richly deserve.

············ A heart filled with praise brings pleasure to God. ············

⁸ to bind their kings with shackles
　　and their leaders with iron chains,
⁹ to execute the judgment written against
　　them.
　　This is the glorious privilege of his
　　faithful ones.

Praise the LORD!

150 ¹ Praise the LORD!

　　Praise God in his sanctuary;
praise him in his mighty heaven!
² Praise him for his mighty works;
　　praise his unequaled greatness!

³ Praise him with a blast of the ram's
　　horn;
　　praise him with the lyre and harp!
⁴ Praise him with the tambourine and
　　dancing;
　　praise him with strings and flutes!
⁵ Praise him with a clash of cymbals;
　　praise him with loud clanging
　　cymbals.
⁶ Let everything that breathes sing praises
　　to the LORD!

Praise the LORD!

147:17 Hebrew *like bread crumbs.* 148:8 Or *mist,* or *smoke.* 149:2 Hebrew *Zion.*

ACKNOWLEDGMENTS

OUR DAILY BREAD WRITERS

NAME	INITIALS	NAME	INITIALS
Dave Branon	JDB	Cindy Kasper	CHK
Anne Cetas	AMC	Albert Lee	AL
Bill Crowder	WEC	David McCasland	DCM
Mart DeHaan II	MRDII	David Roper	DHR
David Egner	DCE	Jennifer Benson Schuldt	JBS
Dennis Fisher	HDF	Joe Stowell	JMS
Vernon Grounds	VCG	Marvin Williams	MLW
Chek Phang Hia	HCP		

PHOTOGRAPHY CREDIT

Sluice copyright © Milan Jurek/SXC. All rights reserved.